The Road to the
White House

F.D.R.: The Pre-Presidential Years

By LORENA A. HICKOK

The Road to the White House

F.D.R.:
The Pre-Presidential Years

CHILTON BOOKS

A Division of Chilton Company
Publishers
PHILADELPHIA AND NEW YORK

To LOUIS McHENRY HOWE
*One of the most devoted and unselfish friends
any man ever had*

Foreword

By ELEANOR ROOSEVELT

This book, THE ROAD TO THE WHITE HOUSE, by Lorena A. Hickok, which tells the story of my husband's life up to the time of his Presidential election, is delightfully written and very easy to read. I think all teenagers will find it providing some additional color to anything they may have learned in their history classes.

I have always believed that biographies are an extremely easy and good way to learn history, and nowadays when biographies are written for different age groups it is quite an art to write so that you will hold the interest of a certain age period. It means picking out anecdotes and explaining personality in a way which will appeal to certain age groups. Miss Hickok has, I think, great facility in her ability to tell a story and make the individual she is writing about alive as a person and appeal particularly to the age group for which she is writing.

I have read so many books for the Junior Literary Guild that I sometimes think I enjoy young people's books almost more than I do those written for the mature reader. But I think it takes a particular gift and perhaps more skill to hold the interest of young people than it takes for those of us who can settle down without much fear of distraction and read a book and not even hear the calls from the world around us which distract all of our youth.

When someone has been written about as much as my husband has been, it must be difficult to find a fresh approach, but I think in this book Lorena Hickok has succeeded in bringing fresh material and fresh interest to a character that should appeal particularly to the young people of our nation, for he had the qualities which she brings out of courage and imagination which mean much to young people.

Author's Note

This book is not a complete biography of Franklin Delano Roosevelt. It takes him only to the threshold of the White House. It is, rather, an attempt to show what made him a President loved and trusted so much by the American people that they elected him to the office four times—a President who led this nation through some of the most difficult and perilous years it had ever known.

A man is, after all, the sum of his background. Circumstances, events, the people around him—all contribute to the growth and the development of his character. His youth, the formative years, have a great deal to do with what kind of man he will be. Hence, the early chapters about a lonely, frustrated teenager at Groton, suddenly transplanted from a secure and happy childhood during which he was the center of the lives of his adoring parents, to a world of adolescents who rejected him because he was "different." All through Groton and Harvard he was concerned chiefly with trying to make a place for himself—to win the respect of his contemporaries.

People make an important contribution. In Franklin Roosevelt's case it was his distant cousin, Theodore Roosevelt, for whom he had a kind of boyish hero-worship which undoubtedly led him eventually into politics himself. There was his wife, whose deep, warm sympathy for the underdog broadened a feeling he had begun to develop at Groton. There was Louis McHenry Howe, whose years of loyal, unselfish devotion helped him to become the astute, realistic politician a man must be if he is to be an effective President. There was also Woodrow Wilson, whose dream of a world in which nations would unite to prevent wars converted a brash young nationalist into a man who would spend all his mature years fighting for international peace.

And there were events. The sudden, terrifying attack of polio which in a few hours changed a vigorous, athletic young man into a cripple, never to walk again without steel braces on his withered legs. The endless hours of pain, endured without complaint by a man who had learned as a schoolboy never to whine or whimper. The long years of patient, heroic effort to walk again—a struggle so gallant that even his political enemies conceded that he was a very brave man.

These are some of the circumstances, people, and events that went into the making of Franklin D. Roosevelt, for twelve years, two months and twenty-two days President of the United States.

LORENA A. HICKOK

Acknowledgments

The author wishes to thank the following publishers for permission to use brief and in one case a number of quotations from books they have published:

Duell, Sloan and Pearce, New York: *FDR, His Personal Letters, The Early Years* (1947), edited by Elliott Roosevelt.

Little, Brown and Company, Boston: *The Ordeal* (1954), second of three volumes of a biography of Franklin D. Roosevelt, by Frank Freidel.

Viking Press, Inc., New York: *The Roosevelt I Knew* by Frances Perkins (1946).

In addition to the aforementioned books, source material for this book was obtained from:

The first and third volumes of Frank Freidel's biography of Franklin D. Roosevelt, published by Little, Brown and Company, Boston: *The Apprenticeship* (1952) and *The Triumph* (1956).

The Democratic Roosevelt, by Rexford G. Tugwell, Doubleday and Company, Inc., New York (1957).

Franklin Roosevelt and the Delano Influence, by Daniel W. Delano, Jr., James S. Nudi Publications, Pittsburgh (1946).

Affectionately, F.D.R., by James Roosevelt and Sidney Shalett, Harcourt, Brace and Company, New York (1959).

The Crisis of the Old, by Arthur M. Schlesinger, Jr., Houghton Mifflin, New York (1957).

A Casual Past, by Francis Biddle, Doubleday and Company, Inc., New York (1961).

Franklin D. Roosevelt, Man of Destiny, by David E. Weingast, Julian Messner, Inc., New York (1952).

The Roosevelt Family, by Karl Schriftgeisser, Wilfred Funk, Inc., New York (1942).

The Harvard Crimson, December 13, 1957, "Franklin D. Roosevelt at Harvard," by Philip M. Boffey.

Harvard Educational Review, Spring, 1961, "The Education of Franklin D. Roosevelt," by Frank Freidel.

The files of the *New York Times.*

A debt of gratitude is due the staff of the Franklin D. Roosevelt Library at Hyde Park for invaluable assistance on research for this book—particularly to Miss Elizabeth B. Drewry, Director; Raymond H. Corry, Curator of the Museum; Miss Margaret L. Suckley, Archivist in charge of the photographs; and William F. Stickle, Photographer, who copied the pictures under trying circumstances while an air-conditioning system was being installed in the Library.

The author also wishes to thank her agent—and friend—Miss Nannine Joseph, and her typist, Jean Hartwig Taylor, who copied the manuscript out of friendship more than for the money she received.

LORENA A. HICKOK

Contents

1

New Boy at Boarding School

He was fourteen years old, five feet, three inches tall, slender, with lively, intelligent blue eyes and a charming smile. His blond hair was neatly parted in the middle—crew haircuts in 1896 were favored only for inmates of penal institutions. He was assigned to the soprano section of the school choir, for his voice had not yet changed. His name was Franklin Delano Roosevelt.

Except for a few weeks at a carefully selected day school in Germany when he was a small boy, Franklin had never before been to school. His education had been supervised by governesses and tutors. One winter he had attended classes, taught by a tutor, in the mansion of Colonel Archibald Rogers, who lived near the Roosevelts at Hyde Park, N.Y., overlooking the historic Hudson River. There were five boys in the class, Franklin, two Rogers boys and two sons of the rector of St. James Episcopal Church, of which Mr. Roosevelt was senior warden.

Franklin was the only child of James and Sara Delano Roosevelt, and until he was sent to boarding school he had never been separated from them for more than a few days. His parents had traveled a great deal and had always taken him with them. He had been to Europe almost every year since he was three, spending months in Germany, France, and England.

The summer before he entered Groton, an Episcopal school for boys, near Boston, Franklin and his tutor had made a bicycle tour of Germany while his parents were staying at a resort in Bad Nauheim. One day they were arrested four times: once for swiping cherries off a branch that hung out over the road, although the tree was behind a stone wall on private property; once because the tutor ran into a goose and killed it; once for wheeling their bikes into a railroad station, and finally for riding into a walled city after sundown. So many things were *verboten* in Germany under the Kaisers! Franklin, whose German was much more fluent than was his tutor's, managed to talk their way out of trouble three times, although they had to pay a fine for swiping the cherries. Even a grim German magistrate couldn't help smiling when Franklin politely reminded him and the farmer that the goose was not a total loss. It could be cooked and eaten!

Up to the time he entered boarding school, Franklin had had a serene and happy childhood. Although he had been given practically everything he wanted—a beautiful Irish setter puppy when he was five, a pony on his seventh birthday, his first shotgun when he was eleven—Franklin was not a spoiled child. Nor was he a "mama's boy," even though his adoring mother did keep him from going away to school at the age of twelve, when most boys in his social group went.

Discipline had never been a problem. His parents did not scold him or punish him for his minor misdeeds. Instead, they reasoned with him and explained why rules must be obeyed, and, since he understood them, the boy accepted them without question. His father and mother

2

treated him almost as though he were an adult, but he was not pampered.

From the time he received his first puppy, he was required to take care of his animals himself. His mother thought it was expecting a good deal of a five-year-old to feed, housebreak, train, and groom a lively setter pup. But his father said:

"I want him to have pets, but he must learn that a dog or a pony is not just another plaything, to be cast aside and forgotten when his attention is attracted to something else. The way to teach him is to make him take care of them himself."

So, although he was only seven when Debby, his pony, was given to him, it became his job to feed and water her, exercise her, groom her, under the watchful eye of Hutchins, the family coachman, and clean out her box stall every day—not an easy or glamorous chore for a small boy.

On one occasion Franklin, frightened and remorseful, accepted without protest discipline that nearly broke his heart. He was twelve years old then. Carrying his precious shotgun, he was walking in the woods with his mother one April afternoon when the gun went off accidentally. He had been carefully instructed by his father on how to handle the gun, with special emphasis on the safety catch. He must always keep it "on safety" until he was ready to shoot. But that afternoon he forgot to check the catch. Fortunately the shot went into the ground, and no one was hurt. He might have killed his mother or himself. For that carelessness, his gun was taken away from him for a year—what seemed to be an interminable period of time.

Franklin was not a lonely child even though, living in the country, being privately tutored, and traveling a great deal, he had few playmates. His one chum was Edmund Rogers, Colonel Rogers' son, and, although they lived a mile apart, he and Edmund played together when Franklin was at home.

When they were quite small they rigged up a platform in a tall tree near Franklin's house, with an old piece of canvas and a toy cannon and pretended they were sailing an American man-o'-war over the seven seas in search of pirates. There was a swimming hole on the Rogers' place, and Franklin and Edmund went swimming there in the summer and skating in the winter. Once they sawed some logs and spent days building a raft. It promptly sank under their weight, but building it had been fun.

Franklin did not miss the companionship of other children, however. He would have told you that his best pal was his father.

James Roosevelt was a widower, fifty-four, when he married one of "the beautiful Delano sisters," Sara, who was half his age. By his previous marriage he had a son, with the odd name of James Roosevelt Roosevelt, who was about the same age as his lovely young bride.

A tall man, with neatly brushed sideburns and eyebrows arched humorously over eyes that crinkled in the corners when he smiled, James Roosevelt was a vigorous man, who loved outdoor life, and his small son Franklin worshiped him. They rode together, hunted and fished together, went coasting and tobogganing down the long steep hill behind their big, old-fashioned frame house set high on a bluff overlooking the river.

The Hudson River, when Franklin Roosevelt was a boy, filled a much more important place, both for recreation and for transportation, in the lives of the families along its shores than it does today. Franklin and his parents sailed, rowed, and canoed on it in the summer. His uncle, John Aspinwall Roosevelt, had an estate not far down the river, and sometimes on warm, quiet summer afternoons Franklin

4

and his parents would go by canoe to Uncle John's house for tea.

In the winter the Hudson was not kept open for navigation, as it now is, but was frozen solidly from shore to shore. It provided wonderful skating and iceboating. Franklin had a small iceboat, and his Uncle John owned the fastest iceboat on the river.

Franklin's father had been a businessman, vice-president of a railroad. By the time Franklin was growing up, however, his father was semi-retired and spent most of his time, when he and his family were not traveling, on his Hyde Park estate. He had all the money he needed, although he was not so rich as Colonel Rogers or his wife's people, the Delanos, whose estate, "Algonac," farther down the river near Newburgh, was one of the show places of the Hudson valley. He was a gentleman farmer who actually made money at it, and he raised trotting horses.

From the time Franklin was a toddler, his father and he would go out after breakfast every morning to look over the farm, an interesting experience for a small boy. Sometimes there would be a newborn calf, baby pigs, lambs, or a little colt. His father was proud of the beautiful old trees on his place, and thus early in life Franklin Roosevelt acquired a love of trees and a knowledge of farming.

Every winter the family would spend a few weeks in New York for the social season and to go to the opera and the theater. When they were in New York, the boy spent most of his time at the Museum of Natural History. One of his most prized possessions was a life membership in the organization, which his Grandfather Delano had given him. At the age of ten he decided to make a collection of specimens of all the birds native to the Hudson valley, shooting only one pair of each kind, and started his own museum. Thus he was presented on his eleventh birthday with a beautiful small-bore English shotgun. Although he lost a year, when the gun was taken away from him, he had in his museum by the time he entered Groton a collection of bird specimens remarkable for a boy of his age.

He was a born collector. While he was still quite small his mother passed on to him a stamp collection that had belonged to her uncle, Edward Delano. For the rest of his life Franklin Roosevelt collected stamps. It was probably his favorite hobby.

While Franklin was still a baby, his father bought a piece of land on Campobello Island, in the Bay of Fundy off the coast of Maine. He built a summer home there, and by the time Franklin entered Groton he had learned to handle his father's big 51-foot schooner, *The Half Moon,* in the tricky tides and currents around the island.

"He's a born sailor," his mother would say, smiling proudly as she watched her son's slender, tanned hands gripping the wheel. "He's a true Delano."

And he was. All of his Delano ancestors, back to the time of the American Revolution, had built ships, owned them, and sailed them. Some had been masters of whaling ships. His Great-grandfather Delano had owned a fleet of clippers that was the envy of the shipping world. They were the fastest ships afloat those days. His Grandfather Warren Delano II had made a fortune in the China trade. Franklin would always remember him as an old gentleman with paralyzed legs, confined to a wheel chair, nodding his approval as the boy read his compositions to him. But in his day, Grandfather Delano had sailed his own clipper ships more than halfway around the world, from New York to Hong Kong.

There was "Fairhaven," the huge, rambling house in Massachusetts, near the wharves where old whalers, out of use since the invention of the marine steam engine, were slowly rotting away. The boy spent hours down there, listening to the bearded, white-haired men who had sailed those ships. For a boy interested in ships and the sea, "Fairhaven" was a real treasure house. It had been built by his Great-grandfather Warren Delano I, and its walls were covered with pictures of ships the Delanos had built and sailed, maps, and navigation charts. Stored in the attic were ancient ships' logs, yellowed with age. One of Franklin's most treasured possessions when he was five years old was a genuine, battered seaman's chest that had come out of the attic at "Fairhaven."

From the time he learned to read, the boy devoured everything he could get his hands on about the sea and ships and the men who sailed them. Long before he went to Groton he knew almost by heart, from reading and re-reading them, a history of the American Navy and a life of Lord Nelson, the English hero of Trafalgar fame.

While his father was an ideal day-time, outdoor companion, his mother entertained him by the hour during the long winter evenings at their home on the Hudson with tales of his seafaring Delano ancestors, and of her own childhood. At the age of eight, Sara Delano, with her mother and six other little Delanos, had sailed all the way down the Atlantic, around the Cape of Good Hope, and up through the Indian Ocean on one of her father's clipper ships to meet him in Hong Kong. From getting her to repeat the story over and over again, Franklin knew the route of that long voyage so well that he practically could have sailed the ship himself! All his life Franklin Roosevelt would say his mother was the best storyteller he had ever known.

It was therefore natural that the slender, blue-eyed fourteen-year-old who, with a homesick lump in his throat, said good-by to his parents in the Rector's study at Groton

School one September evening in 1896, knew exactly what he wanted to be when he grew up. He was going to Annapolis and would become an officer in the United States Navy.

2

Groton

Groton School for Boys, where young Franklin Roosevelt was to spend the next four years, was located in the pleasant, rolling Massachusetts countryside about thirty-five miles north of Boston. The name was and still is pronounced "Grahton."

It was two miles from the tiny hamlet of Groton, where parents used to stay when they came to visit their sons. The boys would hike the two miles to the village to buy toothpaste, pencils and maple sugar, as there was no store at the school.

The school buildings, red brick with white trim, were set around an expanse of lawn—dormitories, a chapel, a gymnasium, and the original building, called "the old schoolhouse" in Franklin Roosevelt's day, where classes were held.

Nearby was the Nashua River, where the boys rowed, canoed, and swam in warm weather and skated in the winter. Off to the north were the New Hampshire hills, called mountains in New England. On the campus were several football and baseball fields and a tennis court.

Groton was one of the most exclusive schools in the

9

country. The tuition was $500 a year, a high fee for the 1890's. Money alone was not enough to get a boy into Groton. His family had to have social prestige as well. Most of the boys were registered for admission when they were babies—Franklin was registered at the age of three. On the board of trustees were names important in the social and financial world, including the elder J. P. Morgan, head of the powerful banking institution known on Wall Street in New York as "the House of Morgan."

A boy was supposed to enter Groton at the age of twelve and spend six years there, finishing when he was eighteen. Franklin entered two years late, partly because his mother couldn't bear to part with him and partly because she thought a boy of twelve was too young to be sent away from home.

The course corresponded to that of junior and senior high school in our public schools. A boy in the lowest grade would be in the seventh grade, and in his last year he would be a high school senior. The classes were called "forms," as they are in the English private schools, and Roman numerals were used—Form I, Form II, and so on, ending with Form VI.

The Rev. Endicott Peabody, the headmaster, was a big, blond, athletic man, who was known as "the Rector" to generations of Groton boys until his retirement in 1940. Groton was an Episcopal school. The boys all attended chapel twice a day, and a great deal of emphasis was placed on what the Rector called "sacred studies."

All of the boys respected the Rector, many were afraid of him, few of them were fond of him—at least while they were at Groton. To be summoned to the Rector's study for some infraction of school discipline was an experience that struck terror in the heart of a Groton boy. The Rector had a truly Jovian temper, which he kept under control most

10

of the time. The object of his wrath, when it did explode, would avoid by all means a second visit to the Rector's study. His attitude toward the boys was usually stern and unbending. He rarely exhibited any sense of humor. Sometimes in letters he would reprimand Grotonians who had long since completed their education and had achieved prominence in business, science or public office.

The Rector had been educated in England, and Groton was modeled after the famous English boarding schools, which are called "public schools," schools such as Rugby, Eton, and Harrow. Its aim was to turn out scholars and gentlemen. Sometimes the boys must have wondered which, in the Rector's estimation, was more important.

It was traditional in England that boys at boarding school should not be pampered and there was no pampering at Groton. Of course, everything possible was done to keep the boys healthy. The school had an infirmary, with a graduate nurse on duty at all times. Often the infirmary would be a very busy place, for if one or two boys came down with mumps or measles, most of the rest of them would catch it, too. The food was plain, but substantial, including very few sweets or rich desserts. Of course the youngsters complained about the food in their letters home, as children at boarding school or camp always do, but undoubtedly their diet was carefully worked out and healthful.

In some other respects the rule against pampering was applied with a heavy hand. While the buildings were attractive on the outside, nothing was done to make them attractive on the inside. The walls and woodwork were painted or varnished in a dull, depressing brown.

It must have been a disconcerting experience to fourteen-year-old Franklin Roosevelt when he was taken to his room to unpack. The boys lived in what were called "cubicles." A cubicle was about six feet wide and nine or ten feet long. It contained a narrow bed, a bureau, a chair, and a small rug. There were no closets, and suits were hung on pegs along the walls.

The walls were about seven feet high, and above them was an open space, extending up to a very high ceiling. A cubicle, opening out into a wide corridor, had no door, only a cloth curtain. At home Franklin had always had his own room. It was a small room simply furnished—he slept in an old-fashioned brass bed—but it had a door, which he could close when he wanted to be alone. At Groton there was no such thing as privacy.

Each dormitory had a large common bathroom, with showers. A boy was required to take a cold shower every morning. For washing up before lunch or dinner there were long, ugly, black soapstone sinks containing tin basins. The boys were given yellow laundry soap to use.

The daily routine began with breakfast at 7:30, followed by chapel at 8:15. Classes started at 8:30 and continued until noon. There were more classes in the afternoon, followed by athletic activities in which every boy was obliged to participate no matter whether he had any ability or not. A Groton boy was supposed to be a manly fellow. Football and baseball ranked at the top, and attendance at a game with another school, like St. Marks, was practically compulsory. For a boy to stay away from a game because he wanted to do something else was considered disgraceful. He showed lack of school spirit, and, to the Rector, lack of school spirit was unpardonable.

A Grotonian was also supposed to be a gentleman. A gentleman, for instance, should know how to carve a turkey at his own table. This they were taught at Groton. Years later, when his own boys were at Groton, Franklin Roosevelt could slice a piece of white meat off a turkey so thin that, as he said, "You could almost read through it!"

For dinner every boy had to wear a dark suit, white shirt with a stiff collar, and evening shoes. In the evening there was another chapel service, followed by a study period in the schoolroom. As the boys filed out at bedtime, they all shook hands with the Rector and Mrs. Peabody and bade them good night. If the Rector smiled slightly and said, "Good night, Jim," or "Good night, Phil," all was well. But if he looked coldly and searchingly at you, and said, "Good night, boy," you were probably in for trouble the next day.

The Groton curriculum also closely followed that of the English boarding schools—Greek, Latin, French, and German, English, mathematics, history, a mere touch of science, "sacred studies," and no economics.

Discipline was strict. An unpardonable breach was to be late. Students were graded on their report cards for punctuality, neatness, and decorum. And a good deal of the discipline was administered by students in the three upper classes—Forms IV, V and VI.

In each dormitory there was a boy, in Form V or VI, who was called a "prefect." At the top there was a "senior prefect," the highest position a Groton boy could achieve. Prefects were selected and appointed by the Rector. Under the general supervision of a teacher (they called them "masters" at Groton) a prefect was supposed to keep the younger boys in his dormitory in line.

For such "crimes" as laziness, lack of school spirit, or failure to show proper respect to upper classmen, the punishment was meted out by the prefects. If the misdeed was serious enough, the culprit was put through an ordeal that would make any boy shake in his boots.

It would begin after evening chapel. The Rector would depart, and the senior prefect would solemnly direct the whole school to remain seated. He would then sternly call out the name of a boy who was to forthwith accompany him to his study. Whereupon a twelve-year-old or a thirteen-year-old would rise shakily to his feet and stumble down the long aisle, with the whole school watching.

In the senior prefect's study, the members of Form VI would assemble and give the youngster a thorough verbal dressing down. They would then shove him out into the corridor, where the boys in Form IV—the fifteen-year-olds —would administer the corporal punishment, usually with an upper-classman holding a stop watch to decide how much mauling the victim could take.

The brutal hazing, for which the English boarding schools were notorious, was not permitted at Groton, but a crowd of fifteen-year-olds roughing up a twelve-year-old can hurt him pretty badly. The Rector and the masters did not interfere. In a way, of course, it was self-government, but at times it was more like mob rule.

One form of punishment was known as "being boxed." In the basement of the dormitory each boy had a wooden box, in which to keep his rough, outdoor boots. The boy would be crammed into the box, and the lid would be shut down. If left there long enough, he could suffocate, which probably accounted for the stop watch in that particular form of punishment.

Certainly the lot of a boy in the first three forms at Groton was neither an easy nor a tranquil one. There are Groton graduates who would tell you that they were all afraid and miserable most of the time, especially the little fellows in Form I. That is probably an exaggeration, but many of them undoubtedly would have been happy to leave "the dear old school" and never return.

A form of punishment known as "black marks" was administered by the masters. A boy could get a black mark for talking or causing any other distraction in the study hall and for a long list of other minor offenses committed while he was under the direct supervision of a teacher. Black marks had to be worked off Saturday afternoons, a half holiday, by doing copying or other chores assigned by the master. Six black marks sent a boy to the Rector's study, an experience to be avoided if possible. A boy who managed to accumulate three or four black marks during a school term was considered a daring fellow and something of a hero by his classmates. If he never got any black marks, he was rated as lacking in that indefinable quality called "school spirit."

Although the Rector, in his contact with the boys, seldom showed any warmth, humor, or real understanding, there were some of their elders whom Grotonians would remember all their lives with pleasure and affection.

One was the Rector's wife. The Rector and Mrs. Peabody lived at the school. They had five daughters and one son.

A Groton institution was "Mrs. Peabody's parlor." There she entertained the boys and visiting parents at tea. All the masters and the boys loved her. She had a way of comforting a homesick twelve-year-old and making him feel a little less lost that made up for her husband's austerity. She had a sense of humor, too, and would take no nonsense from the Rector.

One Grotonian recalls having crossed the Atlantic, years after he had left the school, with the Rector and Mrs. Peabody. He winced, even in his enjoyment, as he heard her say, "Now don't be a stuffy, Cotty!"

And there were some of the masters—in particular William Amory Gardner, whom the boys called "Uncle Billy Wag." Gardner and the Rector were cousins, and the original faculty at Groton had consisted of the Rector, Gardner, and the Rev. Sherrard Billings. The staff had been enlarged considerably when Franklin Roosevelt arrived.

"Uncle Billy Wag" was rich, and he was generous in his gifts to the school. He gave Groton its first chapel and, later, the very beautiful one that is still there. He was a bachelor, but he built himself a large house at the school and kept it staffed with numerous servants. Attached to the house was a huge building, called "the Pleasure Dome," containing a swimming pool, a stage, a squash court, and a maze. Groton boys were invited to his home Sunday afternoons to swim, play games and drink a concoction they called "google"—pink lemonade with plenty of sugar in it. He taught Greek with a sense of humor, to the Rector's disapproval, for his classes were sometimes a bit hilarious. He knew how to pun in Greek!

The Reverend Sherrard Billings was second in command at Groton and took charge whenever the Rector was away. A small man, with a black beard, he had several nicknames, all of them affectionate—"Mr. B," and "Beebs," and "the Little Man." He frequently preached in the chapel, and he taught Latin and Greek.

Another of the masters, Mather Almon Abbott, a Canadian who had been educated in England, later became famous as "Bott," head of Lawrenceville School for Boys in New Jersey. He arrived while Franklin Roosevelt was at Groton, and at first horrified the boys by automatically handing out six black marks apiece. He had not understood the system, but when he found out about it, he publicly apologized to the class and withdrew the black marks. For this he was greatly admired by Franklin and the other boys.

So that was Groton, a school that turned out some very famous men, including a President of the United States. That particular Grotonion spent there what may have been one of the most unhappy years of his life and one which perhaps gave him an instinctive sympathy for the underdog that he never lost.

3

The Outsider

Franklin Roosevelt had looked forward eagerly to going to Groton. Although his childhood had by no means been lonely or unhappy, much of it had been spent with adults and he had the desire, inherent in most human beings, for companionship with his contemporaries.

At Groton there would be boys—many boys, more boys than he had ever known before. Some would be older than he was, some younger. But since he was entering Form III (he would have been a freshman in high school) the other boys in his class would be fourteen-year-olds, as he was.

Franklin had not been there long, however, before he discovered that being a Groton boy was somehow different from what he had expected it to be—different and disappointing.

It was not that he was hazed or mistreated in any way. Except for occasional teasing, which at first he couldn't quite understand, he was simply ignored. And he wanted so much to know the other boys and make friends with them!

To use baseball terminology, Franklin had several strikes against him when he entered the school.

For one thing, the other boys in his class had been together two years. Friendships had been formed. They "belonged." Franklin, a newcomer, would have to find his own place in the group, and, since he had never before associated with many boys, he was a little shy and awkward about it. The other boys didn't need him, and they didn't bother with him.

This disadvantage could have been overcome more easily had he been exactly like the other boys. But in several ways, some of them almost intangible, he was different. In a society of adolescents to be different from the rest of the "crowd" is a miserable experience. Being "different" sets a boy, or a girl, apart, closes doors.

Franklin wore the same kind of clothes the other boys wore: knickers, for fourteen-year-olds did not wear long trousers in those days, long stockings, jacket and vest, a shirt with a starched collar, a necktie. But his suits were cut just a little differently from those worn by the other boys, and they were probably better tailored and fitted him better. They had been made by an English tailor, in London.

Franklin had relatives in England, and he had spent so much time there that he had a slight British accent in his speech. "You don't talk like an American," the other boys would observe scornfully. This made him feel uncomfortable, as though they were accusing him of being a foreigner. Boys at Groton were selected from the American aristocracy, so-called, but none of them could claim ancestry more American than that of Franklin Delano Roosevelt.

As a matter of fact, his ancestors on both sides had come to this country more than one hundred years before the Battle of Bunker Hill. On his mother's side, the de Lannoys, French Huguenots, had migrated to Holland and had given refuge to the English Pilgrims who stopped there before setting out across the stormy Atlantic on their little ship *Mayflower* to the wild, unknown New World. Philippe de Lannoy followed the Pilgrims on the next ship and, along

Franklin Roosevelt, aged 7, on "Debby," his first pony. (1889)

James, Sara, and Franklin Roosevelt, aged 9, on the lawn at Hyde Park. (1891)

Franklin, at 13 (leaning on wheelchair) with his Grandfather Warren Delano and twelve first cousins. (Fairhaven, Mass., 1895)

"Self." (taken by S.D.R.)

Franklin, 14 years old, in 1896 at St. Blasien, France. (In his handwriting is written "Self" taken by S.D.R.—Sara Delano Roosevelt, his mother)

Franklin Roosevelt (*center front*) on the Groton School second football team in 1899.

The serious young man in the straw skimmer is Franklin Roosevelt in 1899 when, at 17. he was manager of the Groton School baseball team.

Franklin, 18 years old (*right*) as *Uncle Bopaddy* in the Groton School play, "The Wedding March," with E. V. R. Thayer as *Poppytop*.

Franklin D. Roosevelt at 18 with his father, James Roosevelt. (Campobello, 1900)

F.D.R. at Hyde Park, just before his 22nd birthday. (January, 1904)

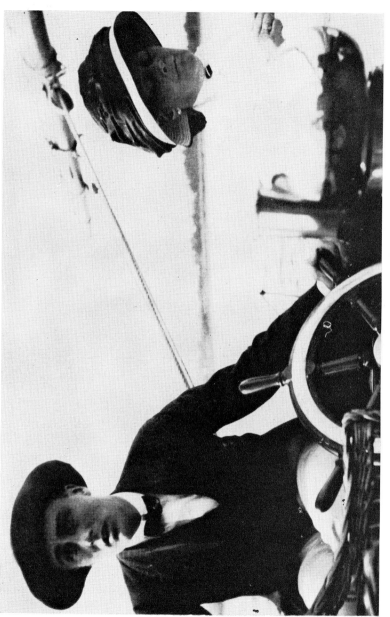

Franklin and Sara Delano Roosevelt, his mother, sailing at Campobello in the summer of 1904, when he was trying to win her consent to his marriage.

Eleanor Roosevelt pho-
tographed by Franklin
during their European
honeymoon in 1905.
Top—In Papadopoli Gar-
dens, Greece.
Bottom—In a gondola in
Venice.

Franklin D. Roosevelt, in 1910, during his successful campaign for the New York State senatorship. He was then 28 years old.

F.D.R., aged 31 years, when he was Assistant Secretary of the Navy. (Washington, D.C., 1913)

Franklin D. Roosevelt in Washington, D.C., July, 1920.

F.D.R., at 38 years of age, with sons James and Elliott on the *Vireo* at Campobello, July 27, 1920.

Governor James M. Cox of Ohio and F.D.R. during their unsuccessful presidential campaign. (Dayton, Ohio, October 19, 1920)

F.D.R. receives a loving-cup from Secretary of the Navy Josephus Daniels on leaving the Navy Department in 1920.

The Roosevelt family with Mamá Sara Delano Roosevelt on the steps of the Campobello house, Summer 1920.

F.D.R. struggles to write his signature after being stricken with polio in 1921. Compare with (*bottom line*) his normally strong autograph nine years later.

Roosevelt and his valet with Dr. William McDonald at Marion, Mass., in 1924. The doctor tried vainly to help F.D.R. to walk without braces.

Governor and Mrs. Franklin D. Roosevelt at Hyde Park. (October, 1930)

President-Elect Franklin Delano Roosevelt and Louis McHenry Howe
reading congratulatory messages. (New York, November 9, 1932)

with Captain Myles Standish, vainly sought the hand of pretty Priscilla Mullins, who married John Alden. Rejected by Priscilla, Philippe married Hester Dewksbury, changed his name to Delano and became Franklin Roosevelt's grandsire, seven generations back.

The first Roosevelt came from Holland, too. He was Claes Martenzsen van Rosenvelt, nicknamed "the Little One." (He was a giant of a man.) He arrived soon after Henry Hudson discovered the river that bears his name and spent years living with the Indians and exploring the headwaters of the Hudson and Delaware Rivers. In 1649 he bought a farm near what is now Battery Park, at the lower tip of Manhattan Island, in New York City, married, changed his name to Roosevelt and became the ancestor of two American Presidents.

From being so much with adults and from spending so much time in Europe, Franklin had acquired manners that adults found charming, but made the boys regard him as a "sissy." For instance, when he shook hands with Mrs. Peabody and bade her good night, he would bow, whereas the other boys would casually, and awkwardly, bob their heads. One of the first lessons in conformity he learned at Groton was not to bow, but to bob his head.

In one respect his manners stood him in good stead. He never had to be disciplined for failing to show proper respect to his elders. To address the Rector, the masters and the young men in Forms V and VI as "sir" came as naturally to Franklin as breathing. There is no record of his ever having been "boxed" or summoned to the study of the senior prefect for a verbal dressing-down followed by mauling from the fifteen-year-olds.

He had still another handicap to overcome. In the form ahead of him was Taddy, his half nephew. Taddy was the son of Franklin's half brother, the man with the odd name,

James Roosevelt Roosevelt. The boy's name was James Roosevelt Roosevelt, Jr., but the family called him "Taddy." The boys at Groton called him "Rosy." Taddy was a big, rather slow-moving boy, who didn't seem to care whether anybody liked him or not. He had the reputation of being lazy and lacking in school spirit. Taddy's mother was a daughter of *the* Mrs. Astor, one of the most famous society leaders New York ever knew. Taddy, his sister, and his father had a house on the Roosevelt estate next door to Franklin's home, but the two boys had never been particularly intimate, partly perhaps because Taddy spent even more time in England than Franklin did.

When the Groton boys wanted to tease Franklin, they called him "Uncle Frank," which certainly did nothing to make him feel comfortable with them!

Wanting so much to "belong," fourteen-year-old Franklin Roosevelt studied the boys who were popular. A sure-fire way to become a hero was to be a star athlete. Football ranked first, then baseball, and third, crew. Franklin had never played football until he went to Groton. He was no good at baseball. And by the time he was in one of the upper forms and eligible for crew, he was too big to be a coxswain, but not heavy enough to pull an oar.

There were things he could do much better than most of the boys at the school. He was an excellent shot, having had a gun since he was eleven years old. He was a good horseman, he played tennis well and could handle any craft from a canoe to his father's big, 51-foot schooner. But those things didn't count at Groton.

All the boys played football. Even the boys in the lower forms had teams that played each other. So Franklin started to learn to play football, with plenty of energy and determination. In his letters home he frequently referred to a banged-up nose, cut lips, and a variety of other bruises.

But he never got beyond the scrub team, even when he was an upperclassman and might have made the first team—called "the varsity" by high-school boys nowadays.

He was terrible at baseball, although all his life he loved to watch a good baseball game. During that first lonely, frustrating year at Groton he wrote his parents jokingly that he belonged to a team called "the BBBB, Bum Base Ball Boys." He said it was made up of the worst players in the school.

Franklin gave up trying to make the school baseball team, but he continued to play football throughout his years at Groton, although there was no glory in it for him—only assorted cuts, sprains, and aches. His mother finally sent him a nose guard to wear.

He was better at track than he was at anything else. As an upperclassman he broke the school record for the high kick. Being a track star wasn't enough, however, to make a Grotonian a hero.

In his studies he ranked high, usually second or third from the top, and he was always graded high for "punctuality, neatness, and decorum." The high grades did not raise his standing among his classmates since some of the most popular boys at Groton barely sneaked through their academic courses.

One thing he did observe. While a boy who had to be disciplined by the upperclassmen for some infringement of the school code was in disgrace, a boy who received a black mark from one of the masters was admired and respected. To Franklin, who in some ways was more mature than his classmates, it seemed rather silly. He had never disobeyed his parents. He had no reason for doing so. But if getting a black mark from one of the teachers would raise his standing—well, why not?

He wrote his parents that he had received a black mark

21

for talking in the study room, adding that he was glad he had done it. "I was thought to have no school spirit," he explained.

One has to read between the lines of his letters home to understand what Franklin Roosevelt was going through that first year at Groton. On the surface, at least, his letters to his parents (and he wrote very often) were cheerful, chatty, and always affectionate. He looked forward eagerly to holidays at home, but all children at boarding school do that. In fact, he apparently never told anyone about his unhappy first year at school until he was a grown man and had finished college. Then he told a few intimate friends and his wife.

But miserable he was, trying hard to fit into the Groton mold and not succeeding too well. In later years he said he had never felt that he really "belonged"—even after he became a prefect and manager of the baseball team. Surely no Groton boy was more enthusiastic than he was when the football team, on which he would have so much liked to play, beat their chief rival, St. Marks, 46 to 0. His letter home started without any salutation:

Nov. 5, 1896
Wednesday

Hurrah Hurrah Hurrah
GROTON
46
St. Marks
0

"I am hoarse, deaf, and ready to stand on my cocoanut!" he added.

Some idea of the fact that Franklin was not very happy may be gained from a statement made, years later, by one of his classmates, James L. Goodwin.

Mr. Goodwin pointed out that Franklin had never been very much with other boys, and that he therefore found it difficult to adjust to boarding school life. As time went on, he noted, and Franklin became an upperclassman, "he developed an independent, cocky manner and at times became very argumentative and sarcastic." This, according to Mr. Goodwin, irritated the other boys considerably. But upperclassmen were not summoned to the senior prefect's study, to be turned over to the boys in Form IV for physical punishment.

It is now a well known fact that cockiness can be a manifestation of an inferiority complex, but neither the boys nor the masters at Groton in the 1890's knew much about psychology.

Edmund Rogers entered Groton with Franklin, but Franklin mentioned his childhood chum less frequently in his letters home than one would have expected. Apparently Edmund had an easier time adjusting himself than Franklin had. Franklin seems to have had to depend for companionship a good deal on Taddy, whose name often appears in his letters, at times with disparaging comments. Although Taddy was a year ahead of him, and a Groton boy was considered "uppity" if he associated with a boy outside his own form, his classmates, who didn't take Taddy very seriously, were apparently so indifferent toward Franklin that it didn't get him into trouble.

Toward the end of his first year, Franklin finally found a friend in his own class. The boy's name was Lathrop Brown, nicknamed "Jake." The two were intimate friends all through the rest of their boyhood and young manhood.

4

Two Roosevelt Clans

On June 4, 1897, as Franklin's first year at Groton was drawing to a close, his fifth cousin, Theodore Roosevelt, who had recently been appointed Assistant Secretary of the Navy by President William McKinley, came to the school to make a speech.

Deeply interested as he was in the Navy, Franklin naturally was strongly attracted to "Cousin Theodore," as he called him in a letter to his parents.

"Cousin Theodore" had had a colorful political career before he became Assistant Secretary of the Navy. He had served in the New York State Assembly, had been a member of the Civil Service Commission in Washington under Presidents Harrison and Cleveland, and had been president of the Board of Police Commissioners in New York City.

As a Police Commissioner he had attained a national reputation. He was a reformer, believed in strict enforcement of the law, and spent his nights touring the city. This did not endear him to the machine politicians, but the public loved him.

"After supper tonight," Franklin wrote his parents, who were in Europe, "Cousin Theodore gave us a splendid talk

24

on his adventures when he was on the Police Board. He kept the whole room in an uproar for over an hour, by telling us killing stories about policemen and their doings in New York."

Apparently the Assistant Secretary of the Navy and his young cousin got on famously, for in his next letter Franklin announced that "Cousin Ted" had invited him to spend the Fourth of July at his home, at Oyster Bay on Long Island, and he had accepted. His parents would be arriving home a few days after the Fourth.

At this point young Franklin, probably for the only time in his life, deliberately disobeyed his parents. They had arranged for him to spend the few days, from the time Groton closed for the summer until their return, with his Delano relatives. His mother apparently wrote back, instructing him to follow their original directions, but Franklin replied that he had accepted Cousin Ted's invitation and expected to go to Oyster Bay—which he did.

Just why his parents objected to Franklin going to Oyster Bay is obscure. For the two Roosevelt clans at that time were on the best of terms. James Roosevelt had met Sara Delano at a dinner party at the home of Theodore Roosevelt's father in New York, where she was visiting her close friend, Corinne Roosevelt, Cousin Ted's sister. And Cousin Ted's younger brother, Elliott, was Franklin's godfather.

The two families were known as "the Oyster Bay Roosevelts" and "the Hyde Park Roosevelts." Cousin Ted and Franklin belonged to the same generation, although Cousin Ted was old enough to be Franklin's father. This was due to the fact that when Cousin Ted was born his father was a very young man, and when Franklin was born his father was past fifty. Franklin's father and Theodore Roosevelt, Sr., Cousin Ted's father, were contemporaries and good friends.

After the Civil War the two clans were also known as the Republican (Oyster Bay) Roosevelts, and the Democratic Roosevelts. They had all been Democrats when Abraham Lincoln ran for President as a Republican in 1860. They all voted for Lincoln in 1860 and again in 1864. But after Lincoln, Franklin's father went back to the Democratic party, while the Oyster Bay Roosevelts remained Republicans. There was never any bitter political disagreement between them, however, until years later, when Franklin and Cousin Ted's son, Theodore, Jr., were both in politics on opposite sides.

While Franklin's parents may have been annoyed with him for disobeying their directions about visiting Cousin Ted on that Fourth of July, they obviously did nothing to prevent him from associating with his Oyster Bay cousins.

During the following Christmas holidays (Franklin was now fifteen and in Form IV at Groton) he went to a dancing party given by Cousin Corinne, who was Mrs. Douglas Robinson. Franklin was dancing with the most popular girl at the party, Cousin Ted's daughter Alice, when he noticed a tall, awkward-looking girl standing all by herself in a corner of the ballroom and half hidden by a rubber plant.

Alice, gay and witty, was wearing a beautiful red party dress. She and all the other girls had grown-up hairdos, and their skirts touched the floor. But although she was taller than any of the others, the girl standing alone was dressed as a child. Her skirts were above her knees, and she was wearing a hair ribbon.

After his partner and he had passed her, Franklin realized who she was. She was his sixth cousin, Eleanor Roosevelt. Her father had been his godfather. Although he had not seen her since they were both quite small, he had heard his mother talking about her. Eleanor's parents had both died, and she was being raised by her very aristocratic and strict Grandmother Hall who rather looked down on the Roosevelts as "tradespeople." Franklin's father and all the other Roosevelts had been businessmen. Eleanor's Grandfather Hall never did a day's work in his life, having inherited a fortune from his parents. So Eleanor rarely saw any of her Roosevelt cousins.

"That poor child," Franklin's mother had said. "Her grandmother insists on keeping her a little girl and dresses her like a child, although she is getting to be a young lady and is very tall for her age."

The dance ended, and Alice's next partner came to claim her. Franklin stood for a moment, thinking. Then he walked over to the tall girl, who looked as though she wanted to cry, bowed low and asked politely:

"Cousin Eleanor, may I have this next dance?"

He was rewarded by a smile that lighted up the girl's plain face and made it beautiful. Franklin knew what it was like to be left out, how it felt not to belong.

As a matter of fact, Franklin's second year at Groton was not so bad as the first year had been. He was learning to conform, to fit into the mold. In one letter to his parents, he wrote that he had received four black marks.

"But I had fun, and it was worth it," he added.

The black marks gave him a kind of self-respect, even though they meant that he had been disobedient, but he was careful, as most of the other boys were, never to get enough so that he had to be sent to the Rector's study. And black marks were given out, after all, for very small, unimportant misdeeds.

He was beginning to stand out in some of the school activities. He was very good, for instance, at debating. He had always enjoyed outdoor sports, and at Groton he learned to ski and to play golf, which he liked very much indeed. His parents sent him a canoe, and, since he handled it expertly, he was given permission to take it out on the river earlier than some of the other boys could.

Franklin's career at Groton almost came to an end, however, near the close of his second year. In February, 1898, relations between the United States and Spain had become strained, sentiment in this country being strongly on the side of the Cubans who were fighting for their independence. On February 15 the U.S. battleship *Maine* was blown up in Havana harbor.

"We heard the news of the *Maine* yesterday, and everyone is much excited," Franklin wrote his parents two days later.

"If the accident turns out to have been done by Spaniards, I think the whole school will take up arms and sail for Spain."

About a month later, the American Navy Department announced that the explosion had been caused by a bomb, set off outside the ship. And for the next few weeks, it was touch and go whether the United States and Spain would go to war.

In his letters home during that period, young Franklin frequently expressed concern about the safety of his parents, who were planning to sail for Europe in April.

"War seems pretty threatening now," he wrote on April 19, the day before his father and mother were to sail, "but I shall not mind it so much when you get to the other side."

The following day he wrote:

"It is rumored today that Spain has sent a squadron of sixty ships against N.Y. and the coast, so you may run right into them and end up in a Spanish prison!

"War is now inevitable, and we are awaiting Spain's reply to our ultimatum. She will of course refuse to leave Cuba, and on Saturday our army is to cross over and invade Cuba. I think, by the time this reaches you, that Cuba will be rid of Spaniards, and Spain will soon be ready to give in."

On April 22, the United States and the country of Spain were at war.

Throughout the preceding weeks, Franklin in almost every letter commented on the situation and expressed concern for his parents' safety. If he had any plans of his own, he did not mention them.

But plans he did have, and he talked his chum, Lathrop Brown, into joining him. On Saturdays and Sundays a vendor of pastries, known as "the Pie Man," used to visit the school with a horse and wagon.

"We'll pay him to drive us to the nearest railroad station, where we can get a train to Boston," Franklin said. "When we get there, we'll go to the recruiting office and enlist in the Navy!"

Lathrop was a little doubtful, especially since Franklin's parents were in Europe.

"What will they think?" he asked.

"Our people will be proud of us, once we get in," Franklin assured him. "I've got to do it. After all, my Cousin Ted is Assistant Secretary of the Navy. What would he think if I didn't do my duty?"

"Maybe they'll turn us down because we're too young," Brown observed.

"Well, I'm sixteen, and I could pass for eighteen," Franklin replied.

"But how could we get out with our baggage?" his friend asked.

"We shan't need any baggage, silly!" Franklin answered impatiently. "They'll give us uniforms as soon as we enlist."

The Pie Man was doubtful, afraid that, if the Rector

found out about it, he'd be barred from doing business at the school.

"Oh, he won't mind, once we're in," Franklin told him. "He's going to be proud of us. We're doing our patriotic duty."

The Pie Man finally agreed to hide the two boys in his wagon the next day, Sunday, and take them to the railroad station. Between them they had very little money, and he demanded all they had except enough to pay their railroad fare to Boston. The boys spent the rest of that day in breathless anticipation.

Toward evening, however, neither of them felt very well. They had no appetite for dinner that night. The following morning, they could hardly get out of bed.

One of the masters, observing them as they appeared at breakfast, ordered them to the infirmary.

"Scarlet fever," the doctor announced. "Put them in with the others."

A couple of cases of scarlet fever had broken out at the school, and the patients had to be isolated.

Apparently Franklin did not have a severe case of scarlet fever, but it was a long, tedious illness. His father and mother hurried home upon receipt of the Rector's cablegram, and Franklin's mother remained at Groton most of the time until she was able to take him home.

Since she was not allowed to enter the room where he was confined, his mother would sit for an hour or longer at a time on top of a stepladder and read aloud to Franklin through the window! Finally he was released, and she took him home to Hyde Park to complete his convalescence.

The school term was nearly over by the time he was able to go back, so he did not return that year. As soon as the hot weather arrived, Franklin and his parents went up to

Campobello for the summer. He must have studied during the vacation, for when he returned to Groton in the fall, he passed all his examinations and entered Form V.

There is no record as to when young Franklin told his parents of the plan he so nearly succeeded in carrying out. But it may be assumed that neither they nor the Rector knew about it until he had finished at Groton!

5

Decision

From the time he was a very small boy dressed in kilts in honor of a distant Scottish ancestor (he detested the kilts and called them "skirts"), young Franklin Roosevelt wanted to be a sailor.

One of his earliest memories was an old sea chanty which his mother sang to him when she was putting him to bed during his babyhood. It went:

Down the river hauled a Yankee clipper,
And it's blow, my bully boys, blow!
She's a Yankee mate and a Yankee skipper,
And it's blow, my bully boys, blow!

Many years later, when Sara Delano Roosevelt was in her eighties, and her son, middle-aged, was President of the United States, they both remembered that song.

By the time Franklin had reached his teens, however, the old whaling ships with their tall masts and the swift and beautiful clipper ships, which his grandfather and his great-grandfather had owned and so proudly sailed were outmoded. Steamships, with engine-driven propellers, had taken their place.

Franklin loved anything that floated, but he could never

get the thrill out of a steamship that he could get out of wind-filled canvas sails. It would no longer be exciting, he thought, to be master of a whaling ship or any other ship driven by great, throbbing steam engines.

However, there was still the United States Navy, and although it no longer sailed under canvas, a career in the Navy could be interesting and filled with adventure. He decided he would like to go to Annapolis. He would need help to get in there. First of all, his grades at Groton must be high, and they were. Next he would have to have a sponsor, someone to recommend him, or "appoint" him, to the Naval Academy. It was possible for the President to appoint a young man to Annapolis or to the military academy at West Point, but most of the appointments were at the disposal of members of Congress. Once granted an appointment, he would have to pass entrance examinations and a rigid physical examination. If he could pass those, he'd be in.

He thought his father could find some Congressman to appoint him, and he is believed to have brought the subject up sometime during the summer after his first year at Groton. James Roosevelt did not immediately turn down his son's request. He agreed that he might be able to help him get an appointment, but he quietly suggested that the decision be postponed for the time being. Franklin would not be old enough to apply for admission to Annapolis until he was in Form VI, his last year at boarding school. His father was so reasonable about it that Franklin accepted his decision without question, and the subject was dropped for the time being.

Franklin brought it up again during the summer at Campobello, following his recovery from scarlet fever. This time James Roosevelt outlined his own plans for his son's future. He had gone to Union College in Schenectady, New

York, and had completed his education at Harvard Law School. He wanted his son to go to Harvard and, after he had received his diploma, stay on there and study law.

"You may never practice law," he said. "I haven't. But whatever your future may be, you will find a thorough knowledge of law very useful. I have."

Going to Harvard and studying law were the two last things in the world young Franklin Roosevelt wanted to do. Next to the Navy, he would have preferred a career in politics, such as his Cousin Ted was having. Soon after the United States entered the war with Spain, Cousin Ted had resigned as Assistant Secretary of the Navy, while Franklin was confined in the Groton infirmary with scarlet fever. He had organized a cavalry regiment, called the "Rough Riders," made up largely of cowboys he had known when, as a very young man, he had been a rancher in North Dakota. Their famous charge up San Juan Hill in Cuba had made "Colonel Teddy" a national hero and had helped elect him Governor of New York. Although Franklin was extremely proud of Cousin Ted, the Navy was still his first choice.

"Life as a Naval officer can be exciting when our country is at war," Franklin's father conceded. "But I've lived through two wars—the terrible Civil War and this last one. War is a bad thing, and I hope we never get into another one.

"In peace time, it wouldn't be the same. You wouldn't be at sea all the time, you know. A good half of your time would be spent ashore, sitting behind a desk. You wouldn't like that much, would you?"

Franklin agreed that it didn't sound very interesting.

"Promotions in the Navy," his father added, "come very, very slowly in peace time. You'd start out as an ensign. Eventually you'd be promoted to lieutenant, junior grade, and after another long wait, you'd become a lieutenant, still a very low rank.

"The higher you would go, the longer you'd have to wait for promotion. Up near the top, you'd have to wait until the man above you was promoted, retired, or died. If you stayed in all your life, you might become a captain or even an admiral. But it would be a long, slow, tedious process."

While Franklin looked thoughtful, his father added:

"Of course, in wartime, it's different. But who wants another war? I don't. You wouldn't want us to go to war and have a lot of fine boys killed just so you could become a high-ranking officer in the Navy, would you?"

Franklin admitted he had never thought of it that way before.

"And if we ever do go to war again," his father said, "you could undoubtedly get a commission in the Navy. With your knowledge of sailing and navigation, it should not be difficult."

Franklin had great respect for his father's judgment and he appreciated his reasonableness. After all, his father hadn't said no. He had only explained the situation to him with great patience and tact. The discussions ended when Franklin finally said cheerfully:

"All right, Pop, Harvard it will be!"

The boy's disappointment about Annapolis was largely wiped out that summer by a gift from his father—a boat of his own. She was a beautiful little twenty-one foot knockabout, with a cabin containing two bunks. She was rigged with a mainsail, jib, and spinnaker. Although he had taken the helm of his father's yacht, *The Half Moon,* many, many times, he could not take her out alone. She was so big she required a crew. But he was a very good sailor and was thoroughly familiar with the dangerous tides and currents around Campobello. So he was allowed to take his own smaller boat out alone. He christened her *The New Moon*.

His best friend, Lathrop Brown, came up to visit him that summer, and the two boys practically lived on the bay aboard *The New Moon*.

They played golf on a nine-hole course that Franklin had laid out. They swam in a little lake on the island because the water in the bay was so cold that no one could stay in longer than a few minutes. And sometimes in the very early morning, they went out on one of the fishing boats.

Franklin Roosevelt's last two years at Groton seem to have been uneventful and fairly happy, on the surface at least, judging by his letters home. Nobody ever said he was a particularly popular boy, but he apparently was respected by his classmates. Although he never learned to play baseball well, in his final year he became manager of the school baseball team, a position of which he was very proud. It was not a particularly glamorous job, since it involved such grubby chores as seeing to it that the playing field was in proper condition and handling all the baggage and other details when the team traveled to another school. Nevertheless, it gave him standing, and he liked that.

In his final year he was given an honor which probably did not mean so much to him, since it came, not from his schoolmates, but was handed to him by the Rector. He became a prefect in charge of the younger boys in his dormitory. Groton usually had eight or ten prefects. The fact that he was made a prefect indicates, at any rate, that the Rector thought well of him.

His letters from Groton do not indicate that Franklin was particularly fond of the Rector, although he respected him. But, as he grew older, finished college, and finally made a success of politics, he apparently had a great deal of respect and a kind of sentimental attachment for the Rector. They wrote back and forth frequently, and Roosevelt sent all of his four boys to Groton.

The first three times Franklin Roosevelt was inaugurated as President, he attended a special service at St. John's, a small Episcopal church across Lafayette Park from the White House. And he always asked the Rector to conduct that service. Even though—whether he knew it or not—the Rector is said to have voted against him the first time he was elected.

Young Man at Harvard

Franklin Roosevelt was eighteen when he entered Harvard in the fall of 1900. He had grown tall, a little over six feet, but he weighed less than 150 pounds. He was handsome, and most of his elders agreed that he had great charm. The general opinion seems to have been that that was about all he had. He was just a well-born young man with nice manners, who was some day to inherit a fortune and become a country gentleman living on his estate at Hyde Park. Already mothers with daughters approaching marriageable age were eyeing him with interest.

There is no indication that he entered Harvard with any eager anticipation. Had he gone to the Naval Academy it would have been different. He had wanted to go to Annapolis, and to have become a midshipman would have fulfilled his boyhood dream. He had agreed to go to Harvard to please his father, it was the accepted pattern for a young man of his social position, and so to Harvard he went— not with resignation, but certainly not with enthusiasm. If, at eighteen, he had any ambitions about his future, he kept them to himself. Nobody would have taken them seriously anyway.

As a Harvard freshman, he followed the course laid out for a boy with his background. He and his Groton friend, Lathrop Brown, moved into a handsomely furnished three-room suite in a section of Cambridge known as the "Harvard Gold Coast." Only boys from wealthy and socially prominent families who had gone to prep schools such as Groton and St. Marks lived on the Gold Coast. They ate at a table set aside in one of the exclusive dining halls for graduates of Groton.

Very few boys whose parents were not well off could go to Harvard, although a small number managed to work their way through, waiting on table, tending furnaces, shoveling snow, mowing lawns and, after they became upperclassmen, doing some tutoring. Most of the students came from prep schools in the West or South, less exclusive and not so well known as Groton. Many came from the public high schools. They lived in old, rather run-down dormitories around "The Yard," as the campus was called. Their only contact with the Gold Coast boys was in the classrooms and, in a few instances, on the athletic fields. Not even the Gold Coast boys could keep a star football player down!

For most of the Gold Coast boys the academic advantages offered by Harvard held little interest. At Harvard those days "C" was considered "a gentleman's average," and Franklin conformed to the pattern. He could have done much better, for he had a quick, intelligent mind. During his years at Harvard he studied under some of the most distinguished professors in the world, but there is no indication that any of them exerted any great influence over him. He did manage to acquire a good cultural background, but it must have been largely by saturation, with very little effort on his part. He never rose above a "C" average.

As a freshman at Harvard he started immediately to follow the course he had followed at Groton, trying to establish a place for himself, to win the admiration and respect of his classmates. His first choice was football. He was still too light to be a football star, however, and he never got beyond the freshman scrub team.

Franklin's college career was interrupted in the early winter of his freshman year by a family sorrow that was to have a lasting impact on his future, although neither he nor anyone else realized it at the time. His father, aged seventy-two, had been suffering from heart trouble for several years. That autumn his health began to fail noticeably, and Franklin's letters home were filled with concern about him.

Franklin's mother had rented a house at Aiken, South Carolina, hoping that a winter in a warm climate might help her ailing husband. Aware as he was of his father's illness and worried about it, Franklin apparently did not realize how serious it was. For in one letter he assumed that his father would take Bobby, his favorite saddle horse, down to South Carolina.

But James Roosevelt was no longer able to ride Bobby, and he never made it to Aiken. In November his wife took him to New York, where he could be under the constant supervision of their family doctor. Franklin's last letter to "My dearest Mama and Papa" was written on December 3. A day or so later he received a telegram summoning him to New York. James Roosevelt died on December 8 in the family's apartment. His wife and his two sons were with him.

Franklin's own grief at the loss of his father had to be pushed into the background as he tried to comfort his mother. He did not return to college until after the Christmas holidays, but remained with her in the big house at Hyde Park that now seemed to both of them so empty and desolate.

Since Franklin was still a minor, his share of his father's estate was left in trust, and his father had stipulated in his will that Franklin's mother should be his sole guardian, with complete supervision over him. Most of the estate was left outright to her, and this, with the fortune she had inherited from her father, made her a very wealthy woman.

Franklin's share of the estate, after it came to him on his twenty-first birthday, never gave him an income of much more than $5,000 a year. The result was that for many years, especially after he was seized with infantile paralysis, he had to depend a good deal on his mother's generosity.

His mother took very seriously her husband's instructions that she was to be their son's sole guardian, and she was never able to let go. This tendency on her part, together with his partial dependence on her financially— though she was very generous—led her to dominate her son and her daughter-in-law for years, creating a difficult situation for them.

His father's death also tended to increase the influence his boyhood hero, Cousin Ted, had over Franklin. Cousin Ted in the autumn of 1900 ran for Vice-President with the victorious William McKinley, and when Franklin returned to college for his sophomore year, McKinley had been assassinated, and Theodore Roosevelt was President of the United States. He was fond of Franklin, and it was natural that the young man, greatly admiring his distinguished cousin, should look up to him almost as to a second father.

A boy of eighteen may suffer keenly the death of a beloved parent, but youth rebounds more quickly than does middle age. Presently Franklin was back at Harvard, absorbed in his own activities, while his mother wandered in lonely desolation between Hyde Park and New York. Franklin wrote her tenderly, on paper with a heavy black border, but his letters were briefer and less frequent than they had been while he was at Groton. During his sophomore year, his mother rented a house in Boston to be near him.

Franklin still had ambition to become a star athlete, although it was obvious that he would never make the varsity football team. He decided to try crew, which ranked second in importance to football. The Harvard-Yale boat race was almost as much of an event as the Harvard-Yale football game. As soon as the ice was out of the River Charles the following spring, he began spending long, exhausting hours practicing. In this effort he failed also, although he did stroke one of the club crews. He never made the varsity.

Looking about for some other activity in which he might excel, Franklin, upon his return to college after his father's death, decided to try for a place on the staff of the *Harvard Crimson,* the daily newspaper edited and published by the students. Every year freshmen were invited to compete for positions on the staff, and there were many applicants.

A freshman applicant was turned loose on the campus to bring in all the news he could collect. He had to be intelligent, fast on his feet, and willing to work. Sometimes he would put in as much as six hours a day—and this on top of his studies. Franklin went at it with characteristic enthusiasm.

There is a story, told by most of his biographers, that Franklin Roosevelt obtained a position on the staff by bringing in the biggest scoop the *Crimson* had had in years. William McKinley, Republican, was running for President in 1900 against William Jennings Bryan, Democrat. According to the story, young Franklin went to the home of Harvard President Charles W. Eliot and asked him how he was going to vote.

Very few freshmen would have had the temerity to go to see President Eliot, let alone to ask him how he was going to vote. Also he made it a rule never to grant interviews to *Crimson* applicants. President Eliot is supposed to have been so taken by surprise at the young man's brashness that, after reprimanding him, he said drily: "You may say that I shall vote for Mr. McKinley." The story was picked up by the wire services and appeared on page one in newspapers all over the country.

The story is true all right, except in one respect. Franklin Roosevelt didn't get the interview! In the Franklin D. Roosevelt Library at Hyde Park there is a memorandum, dictated by the late President himself, stating that it was another boy, not he, who accomplished the feat.

During the second semester of his freshman year, however, Franklin Roosevelt did get a smaller scoop that undoubtedly helped him to win one of the coveted positions on the *Crimson* staff. In the late winter Cousin Ted, Vice-President at that time, arrived in Cambridge to visit his friend, Professor Lowell of Harvard. Franklin telephoned him, was greeted cordially by Cousin Ted and learned that the Vice-President was going to speak to Professor Lowell's class in Government the following morning. The *Crimson* editors and everybody else were delighted, with the possible exception of Professor Lowell, whose class must have been riotous that morning, for practically the entire student body fought to get in!

Except for a brief interval, while he was trying to become an oarsman in the spring of his freshman year, the *Crimson* was Franklin's chief interest while he was at Harvard. He spent hours working for it when he might have been reading for the courses he was taking.

While he was never particularly popular with the Gold Coast boys, young Franklin Roosevelt, with his good looks, charm, money, and family background, was much sought after socially, both in Boston and in New York. During his freshman year he attended no parties, because he was in mourning for his father, but in the following years, he lived a very active social life. As any boy would, he enjoyed good times, parties, and pretty girls. Also, his mother would have been very much disappointed had he not accepted the many invitations he received. Parties, however, were of secondary interest. *The Crimson* came first.

When Franklin entered his sophomore year, Theodore Roosevelt had become President and before long had inaugurated his Square Deal and was happily engaged in "trust busting," breaking up the huge business combines that were running the country. This made him exceedingly unpopular with the rich, whose sons lived on the Harvard Gold Coast. They called him "a traitor to his class," as years later the big business leaders would refer to Franklin Roosevelt with his New Deal.

Franklin, naturally, stoutly defended Cousin Ted, which did not make him any more popular with his Gold Coast associates. They called him a "radical." His arguments with the Gold Coast boys may account for the fact that he was not asked to join Porcellian, swankiest of all Harvard clubs, although Cousin Ted had belonged to it when he was a Harvard student. Franklin did make Fly, the second most exclusive club, Hasty Pudding, and a number of others, including the Political Club, in which he became very active. He became librarian for Fly and Hasty Pudding, and, while shopping around for books for the club, he began to acquire for himself the naval prints that would one day become the largest and most valuable privately owned collection in the world.

In his sophomore year he managed to annoy his Gold Coast associates by doing something that had no connection with the college. The Boers, the white settlers in South Africa, had lost their war for independence from the British, and thousands of them were destitute. Franklin Roose-

44

velt headed a committee to raise money for relief for the Boers. The other residents of the Gold Coast had been, almost to a man, on the side of the British.

Most of the papers he wrote while studying English composition were just about what one might have expected of a young gentleman of his financial and social standing, but he wrote one that gave some evidence of the type of man he was eventually to become. In it he advocated the admission of Negroes to Southern white colleges and universities as they were admitted to Harvard.

Franklin was twenty-one, and a Harvard senior, when in 1904 Cousin Ted ran for his second term as President, heading the Republican ticket. Franklin cast his first presidential vote for Cousin Ted, although Franklin's father had been a Democrat, and he regarded himself as a Democrat too.

7

Courtship

During the late winter of his junior year at Harvard Franklin began courting his sixth cousin, Eleanor Roosevelt, Cousin Ted's niece.

He had seen her a few times after Cousin Corinne's party, where he had asked her to dance. But as he was entering his last year at Groton, she had been sent to a girls' boarding school in England, where she had remained three years. When Franklin saw her again she was eighteen and one of the most unhappy debutantes ever introduced to New York society.

Eleanor had been happier at school in England than she had ever been before in her life. Elderly Mlle. Souvestre, the headmistress, had been able to see beneath the surface —Eleanor was almost six feet tall, still gawky and homely, with prominent front teeth, like her Uncle Ted's. Mlle. Souvestre had found the girl highly intelligent, quick to respond to her proffered friendship and very lovable when she was not feeling shy and ill at ease. During the summer vacations she had taken Eleanor with her all over Europe, and they had had wonderful times together.

But at the end of her third year, her Grandmother Hall and her aunts decreed that she must come home and make her debut. In the high society in which the Halls and the Roosevelts moved, it was unthinkable that a girl should fail to "come out," as they put it, when she was eighteen. Eleanor would be eighteen that fall. She accepted the ruling, even though she was miserable about it. Timidly, and without any real hope, she asked her grandmother if she could go to college, and she got what she expected, an unqualified no.

Eleanor's mother, Anna Hall, had been one of the most beautiful and popular debutantes New York society had ever seen. All three of her mother's sisters, the two youngest of whom were not very much older than Eleanor herself, were great beauties too, as her grandmother had been when she was a girl. All Hall women were supposed to be beautiful. Overly conscious of her own lack of looks, Eleanor felt that she was a disappointment to her grandmother. And the fact that her aunts called her "the ugly duckling" and seemed to take it for granted that she would never find a husband made her feel even worse. She had lovely clothes, given to her by a rich aunt, but they didn't help.

Another disadvantage was that, except for her brother, who was much younger than she, and on the rare occasions when she saw her Roosevelt cousins, Eleanor had never associated with boys. She could talk well and interestingly to people with whom she felt comfortable. But whenever she met a young man at a party, she would be stricken dumb. Since she was not pretty and couldn't talk, the young men were not interested in her. At her coming-out party only one man had asked her to dance, and he had been a friend of her parents and one of her Uncle Ted's Rough Riders, although he was not a cowboy but a member of a very aristocratic Scottish family. She had left her first ball before midnight and had slunk wretchedly into her grandmother's New York town house.

Handsome, much more self-assured than he had been as a Groton boy, a prominent Harvard man, Franklin Roosevelt was invited to many parties in New York, as well as in Boston. Some day he would inherit a fortune from his mother, and girls looking for husbands were as interested in him as were their mothers.

Naturally Eleanor was surprised and delighted when one night at a party, to which she had dragged herself with a heavy heart, she saw a tall, good-looking young man coming toward her, smiling. It was Cousin Franklin!

"Welcome home, Cousin Eleanor," he said. And he added with a grin: "May I have this next dance?"

As they danced together she found herself, to her surprise, telling him about school in England, Mlle. Souvestre and the trips they had taken together. Franklin listened with interest, asking just the right questions. He brought over some of his Harvard friends to meet her, and, with Cousin Franklin at her side, she discovered that she could talk to them too. It was the first party she ever enjoyed.

Franklin was a busy young man at Harvard those days. But his studies weren't taking up very much of his time. He was critical of the courses he was taking, in sociology and history. He complained to his roommate, Lathrop Brown, that they were too "artificial," that they had no connection with "the realities of life." An observation rather typical of a twenty-year-old, who thinks he knows all about life! But even without trying very hard and never getting more than a "C" average, he had accumulated enough credits by the end of his junior year so that he could have received his diploma a year ahead of his class. He decided to stay on another year, however, taking advanced courses in English, history, and economics.

"The courses will do me a lot of good, whether I get a "B" or a "D" in them," he wrote his mother. "To do the former would make me work so hard that I could not do justice to my senior year."

"Doing justice to his senior year," to Franklin, meant spending most of his time working on the *Crimson*. He had become president of the *Crimson,* a position of high honor on the campus.

It was his job to write the editorials, and, as an editorial writer, he took up causes that certainly did not add to his popularity on the Gold Coast.

For one thing, he stirred up interest among the rest of the students in voting in the class elections. And he succeeded in getting some boys who did not live on the Gold Coast to run for office. He was not entirely successful, but the Gold Coast boys were surprised and irritated by the competition. Young Franklin Roosevelt was bringing democracy—with a small "d"—to the Harvard Campus.

Another of his campaigns annoyed the Harvard Overseers, as the trustees were called. The old dormitories, in which most of the students lived, were without fire escapes. In case of fire, the only way they could get out was down flimsy wooden staircases. Some of the boys kept coils of rope in their rooms! The Overseers didn't want to spend the money, but the brash young editor of the *Crimson* stirred up such a commotion that they finally had to build fire escapes.

In spite of all his activities at Harvard, Franklin began accepting more and more invitations to parties in New York, because the more he saw of his Cousin Eleanor, the more interested he became in her. Bored with society, she had taken a job as a volunteer in a Lower East Side settlement house. Franklin was entirely in sympathy with her program. He himself had somehow managed to spend a good deal of time while at Harvard working with a boys' club in a poor section of Boston.

Courting a girl in the social circle in which the two of them moved was not easy. They were supposed never to see each other without a chaperon. But Franklin somehow managed things so that he could call for Eleanor at the settlement house and escort her home. Once she took him to see a child with whom she was working. The child was ill, and young Roosevelt found himself climbing flights of rickety stairs in one of the worst tenement houses on the Lower East Side. His expression was conscience-stricken as he said to her later:

"I never had any idea that *anybody* had to live that way."

Before the end of his junior year, he knew he was in love with Eleanor, and in December, 1903, near the end of the first semester of his fourth year at Harvard, he told his mother he planned to marry her.

The shock staggered Sara Roosevelt. With an eagle eye, she had watched other girls (much more attractive on the surface) playing up to her adored son. But it had never occurred to her to worry about Cousin Eleanor—"the poor child." She was so plain and so shy. With Cousin Eleanor she had felt that her boy was safe, no matter how often he was seeing her. Even a pathetic little letter from Eleanor failed to placate her.

From the home of her Cousin Susie (Mrs. Henry Parish, wife of a New York banker) with whom she was then living, Eleanor wrote:

"Dearest Cousin Sally,

"I must write you and thank you for being so good to me yesterday. I know just how you feel and how hard it must be, but I do so want you to learn to love me a little. You must know that I will always try to do what you wish for I have grown to love you very dearly during the past summer.

"It is impossible for me to tell you how I feel toward Franklin. I can only say that my one great wish is always to prove worthy of him.

"I am counting the days to the 12th, when I hope Franklin and you will both be here again, and if there is anything which I can do for you, you will write me, won't you?

"With much love, dear Cousin Sally,

"Always devotedly,

"Eleanor."

Eleanor had visited Franklin and his mother at Campobello the preceding summer, and Sara Roosevelt, all unsuspecting, had welcomed her there with open arms!

Franklin wrote his mother tenderly:

"Dearest Mama—I know what pain I must have caused you and you know I wouldn't do it if I really could have helped it. . . . I know my mind, have known it for a long time and know that I could never think otherwise. Result: I am the happiest man just now in the world; and the luckiest.—And for you, dear Mummy, nothing can ever change what we have always been and always will be to each other—only now you have two children to love and to love you—and Eleanor, as you know, will always be a daughter to you in every true way."

The letters had no effect on Sara Roosevelt's determination not to permit her son to marry Eleanor, or anyone else, at that time. For four years, ever since his father's death, she had looked forward to having him at home with her, all to herself, at Hyde Park. She wasn't going to give up easily.

She proceeded to do what so many parents try to do under similar circumstances. She tried to break it up.

The method she chose was to take Franklin and his roommate, Lathrop Brown, on a six weeks' Caribbean cruise the following February and March; but to no avail. In her diary she noted that Franklin seemed "blue."

Announcement of the engagement was delayed for a year while she hoped against hope that Franklin would get over what she chose to think was a case of boyish, puppy love. "Why, they're just children!" she told herself over and over again. Franklin was twenty-one in January after he told his mother of his engagement. Eleanor had reached her nineteenth birthday the preceding October.

Sara couldn't break it up, so she decided to take charge. Eleanor—insecure, unsure of herself—was easy prey. Thus she permitted her mother-in-law to dominate her completely for years. Mamá, as they called her, held the purse strings, although nobody ever accused her of not being generous.

8

Society Wedding

Franklin Roosevelt's mother and his sweetheart watched proudly as he received his Harvard diploma in June, 1904. He was not graduated with honors, however, nor did he make that august and scholarly fraternity Phi Beta Kappa, although years later he was given an honorary membership in it.

It is to be doubted whether any of his professors or his classmates expected him to have a distinguished career, even though his teachers observed that he had a quick, intelligent mind. Nor did his mother or his bride-to-be expect any particular distinction of him. His mother hoped he would take his place in New York society and spend most of his time at Hyde Park, as his father had done. To Eleanor, it didn't matter what he did, as long as he was happy.

She spent part of that summer at Campobello. Since she was not permitted to travel without a chaperon, she arrived accompanied by a personal maid. She and her fiancé had little opportunity to be alone together. His mother was sweet to her—with that kind of surface sweetness a woman can display toward another woman she resents.

Barely hidden under every polite, kind remark there would be a barb. Sensitive, perceptive Eleanor meanwhile tried her best to please "Cousin Sally" and to win her love.

In the autumn Franklin entered law school at Columbia University in New York—rather unwillingly. He probably would have preferred to take a master's degree at Harvard in government, political science, or history. His reluctant decision to study law was probably due in part to his promise to his father, of which, one may be certain, his mother reminded him. Also, had he remained at Harvard, he would have been separated most of that year from the girl with whom he was so much in love.

He couldn't have been a very good student at law school that year. As it was, seeing Eleanor alone was not easy even though they were engaged. They went to many parties, but Eleanor was always chaperoned. He could not call on her if Cousin Susie was away. They were allowed to go to church together, and sometimes, on Sunday afternoon walks in Central Park, they were chaperoned by Eleanor's young brother, Hall, then a student at Groton. For a girl brought up as Eleanor was, to lunch or dine alone with a young man in a restaurant was out of the question.

In December, a year after he had told his mother of his plans, she finally gave in, and the engagement was announced. They planned to be married in the spring, but the date had to be set at a time convenient for Eleanor's Uncle Ted, now "Uncle" Ted to Franklin too, who wanted to give the bride away. Uncle Ted was about to enter his second term as President of the United States. They settled on March 17, since Uncle Ted was coming to New York that day to review the St. Patrick's Day parade.

Inaugurations those days occurred on March 4, and Franklin and Eleanor were present to see Uncle Ted sworn in. Visiting the White House was no novelty to either of them. Eleanor was the President's favorite niece and had stayed at the White House several times. Uncle Ted was also fond of Franklin, and he, too, had been a White House guest. But this occasion, with all the glamour—flags and bunting everywhere, bands, the cheering crowds, the big parade, witnessed by Uncle Ted and his relatives from special stands set up in front of the White House—was something special.

"We've seen history in the making today," Franklin solemnly assured his bride-to-be. If it ever occurred to either of them that Franklin himself might some day stand where Uncle Ted stood, on a platform at the East Portico of the Capitol, they didn't mention it. It is unlikely that the thought ever entered their minds. Franklin (as much as he admired Uncle Ted) had not yet decided what he wanted to do, beyond marrying Eleanor and finishing his law course, and Eleanor, at that time, wasn't even mildly interested in politics.

Their wedding took place at Cousin Susie's house in New York since Grandmother Hall had closed her New York house and was living on her estate at Tivoli, near Hyde Park. Because of Uncle Ted's presence, it turned out to be one of the oddest weddings ever held in New York society.

Cousin Susie's house, on the fashionable East Side, was only a few doors from Fifth Avenue, and the wedding march was nearly drowned out by brass bands blaring forth "The Wearin' o' the Green," as the Irish marched up the avenue. Uncle Ted was able to leave the reviewing stand only long enough to give the bride away and have a piece of wedding cake.

A President of the United States is always followed by crowds, so the streets in front of Cousin Susie's house, and for blocks around, were packed with people, all chanting:

"We want Teddy! We want Teddy!" A President is also accompanied by Secret Service men and police to protect him. In the confusion that day, Franklin himself had some difficulty getting into the house. Some of the invited guests never got in at all, and there were a good many gate-crashers. Uncle Ted arrived looking a bit disheveled, wearing on his lapel a large bunch of wilted shamrocks.

But the tall, slender bride, in her heavy white satin gown with a long train and a veil of priceless Brussels lace that had been worn by her mother and her grandmother (and was kept in a bank vault between weddings) looked every inch a princess. She appeared to be entirely oblivious of the commotion, and the expression on her face was radiant. Lathrop Brown, Franklin's Groton chum and Harvard roommate, was best man, and Cousin Ted's daughter, known all over the country as "Princess Alice," was maid of honor. The bridesmaids, several lovely debutantes, were beautifully costumed. Dr. Endicott Peabody performed the ceremony.

After it was over, Uncle Ted kissed the bride, congratulated her on keeping the Roosevelt name in the family, and hurried off into the library, where refreshments were being served. It was quite natural for everybody to be more interested in the President than they were in the bride and groom, and presently Eleanor and Franklin found themselves standing quite alone. Even the receiving line had disappeared. Eleanor was a little worried, thinking Franklin's feelings might be hurt, but he thought it was funny, laughed, and suggested that they join the crowd.

They spent a few days at Hyde Park—apparently Franklin's mother remained in New York—came back to the city, moved into an apartment hotel, and Franklin resumed his studies at Columbia. Their real honeymoon was postponed until the university closed for the summer.

Their wedding trip, which lasted all summer, was a grand tour of Europe—Italy, the Alps, Germany, Paris, London, rural England and Scotland, where they both had relatives. They bought things they liked. Franklin added to his collection of naval prints. They bought furniture, too, linens, lace and, in Venice, many yards of beautiful red damask. It wore well, that red damask—Mrs. Roosevelt still had some small red chair cushions covered with it in her New York apartment years after her husband had died. In Scotland they purchased the first of a long succession of Scotty dogs. They named him Duff, and brought him home with them.

Wherever they went, there were people who thought the amiable, good-looking and apparently wealthy young bridegroom was President Theodore Roosevelt's son, instead of being merely his sixth cousin and his niece's husband. For this reason, they received a good deal more attention than would have been lavished upon them ordinarily. In London, for instance, they found themselves installed in the royal suite of a swank hotel. Franklin wrote his mother humorously that the suite was so big that they had difficulty finding their way around in it and added that it was, of course, away beyond what they could afford. Whereupon, his mother undoubtedly sent him a check.

Some English newspapers of the time, now on file in the Franklin Roosevelt Library, show pictures of the young couple with captions that read "President Roosevelt and Bride on Honeymoon."

There were other funny and, at times, embarrassing incidents. Once, while they were visiting some of their relatives who owned a beautiful country estate in England, Eleanor was invited to speak at the opening of a garden show. Eleanor, who had never made a speech, declined in terror, and her husband took her place. Even Eleanor, who had never cooked a meal in her life, joined in the general amusement as she heard her husband solemnly assuring a group of English housewives that vegetables should always be cooked in milk.

But she wasn't amused, only humiliated, when one of her husband's English relatives, member of a family prominent politically, as well as socially, asked her: "What is the difference between the federal and state governments in your country?" Eleanor didn't know. Red-faced she was frantically trying to think of an answer, when Franklin, who had overheard the question, came to her rescue.

Her worst time, though—one of the most unhappy evenings she ever spent in her life—came when they were dining with some of her husband's friends in London. After dinner, they played cards for money. The stakes were not at all high, just enough to make the game interesting. Eleanor Roosevelt had never gambled, considered it immoral, and refused to play for money. Everybody was astonished, they looked at her as though they thought she was an idiot, and her card partner was annoyed with her. Whatever his own feelings might have been, her husband did not reproach her, but she undoubtedly apologized to him for days thereafter. That evening, however, Franklin Roosevelt discovered something about his shy, usually docile bride that he had not suspected before. When a matter of principle was involved, she could be as stubborn as any Dutchman who ever lived. After all, she was a Roosevelt too!

When they finally returned to New York, they found that Franklin's mother had rented and furnished a small house for them. It was an attractive house, beautifully furnished, but except for adding her wedding presents and some of the things she and Franklin had bought in Europe, the young bride had had nothing whatever to do with its decoration. It wasn't really her home; it was her mother-in-law's idea of the kind of home her adored son should have.

Eleanor didn't know it then, but it would always be that way. Later her mother-in-law spent a small fortune on a big double house on 65th street, near Park Avenue, with sliding doors in between. Franklin was dumfounded when, in the evening after they had moved in, he found his wife sitting at her dressing table crying. Through her tears she tried to explain to him that she wanted a home of her own, furnished as she wanted to furnish it. He was very patient and reasonable with her, but he could not understand her. If his mother chose to give them a beautiful house—well, why not accept it gracefully? It would at least, he probably thought, make his mother happy and help keep peace in the family.

Franklin Roosevelt loved Hyde Park, the house where he had spent such a happy childhood. He regarded the estate as home, as did his children, but it wasn't his home or his wife's home really—it was his mother's home, and so long as she lived, Sara Roosevelt sat at the head of the table in the dining room of the big house at Hyde Park, her son at the foot and her daughter-in-law on the side.

Eleanor had an income of her own, from her parents' estate, and between them when they were first married, she and her husband had about $12,000 a year, ample for their needs before the children started coming. Franklin's mother thought otherwise. Her checkbook was always open. Her daughter-in-law was supposed to be completely subservient to her wishes in matters of money as well as otherwise.

She always referred to her son and his wife possessively as "my children." And when she said it to some of their friends of whom she did not approve, it sounded disconcerting—if not downright insulting.

Bored Young Attorney

Franklin Roosevelt's honeymoon could have been marred by one unpleasant piece of news. While he was in Europe he received word that he had flunked two of his law courses at Columbia.

He did not let it spoil his good time, however. Undoubtedly he was less bothered by it than most young men would have been. After all, he had gone to law school because it was expected of him and possibly because he had not made up his mind what he really wanted to do.

Whatever he was thinking he kept to himself. A habit he had acquired during the years at Groton, of not revealing his doubts, his perplexities, his dreams or his troubles to any one, had become fixed. He had never whimpered.

His relations with his mother had grown less and less intimate. "I don't know what is in his mind," she would say plaintively. "He never tells me." His attitude toward her was gay, affectionate, and grateful. If she tried to get too close, a curtain would drop.

He returned to Columbia that fall, reviewed the two courses, passed the examinations and went on with his studies. For the rest of the two remaining years he was there, he maintained an average about as high as he had at Harvard. Never at either university did he get grades as high as he had received at Groton.

In the meantime, he was enjoying life. The Roosevelts were popular in the young New York social set and entertained charmingly in their well-staffed, attractive home. By the end of the winter, however, they were going out less, for their first baby was on the way. She arrived in May, a blonde, blue-eyed little girl, whom they named Anna Eleanor, after her mother. They called her Anna. While she was delighted with her beautiful baby, as any young mother would be, Eleanor felt guilty. She knew her mother-in-law wanted a boy, to be called James, after his grandfather. There was no reason for her to worry, for James arrived when Anna was about a year and a half old.

Immediately Mamá took charge. Eleanor was only the children's mother. They were *her* children. Never, while her children were small, was Eleanor Roosevelt permitted to hire her own nursemaids. Mamá hired them—stiff, starched, English nursemaids, whose attitude toward the mother of their young charges was apt to be somewhat condescending.

If her husband noticed such things, he did nothing about them. He may not have noticed them, for Eleanor was not the complaining type. After all, he had fought one big battle with his mother and had won—he had married the girl he wanted to marry. From then on, it must have seemed to him, the sensible course to follow was to humor his mother and keep peace in the family. And during those early years his wife quietly followed his wishes, except for rare outbursts.

He completed his law course in 1907, but did not bother to take his degree. Without any difficulty he passed his New York State bar examinations. His family connections may have had something to do with the fact that he was taken on as a law clerk by one of the most highly respected and successful legal firms in New York. He had to work for a year without pay, but their combined incomes, plus his mother's frequent checks, made it possible for the young Roosevelts to live very comfortably.

Being a law clerk is a dull enough job even for a young man who is serious about making a success in the legal profession. The status of law clerk is only a notch or two above that of office boy. He runs errands, looks up references in law books, carries the boss's brief case when they go to court. After he has been a law clerk for a year he becomes a practicing attorney employed by the firm. He is given more important research work to do, is sometimes described as "an attorney of record"—and still on occasion carries the boss's brief case to court. Sometimes he is permitted to represent the firm in very minor court actions. The firm with which Franklin was associated, however, specialized in corporation law and lower court cases were seldom a part of its practice.

Franklin obviously was not interested in the job even after he began to receive a salary. Occasionally he would get so lax that the head of the firm would have to jack him up.

What was going on in his mind may have been revealed by a joking remark he made one day to some of his fellow law clerks as they were sitting around the office.

"Some day," he said with a grin, "I'm going to be President of the United States."

They thought he was joking, and he very likely was. Or it may have been a trial balloon. Whichever it was, only Franklin Roosevelt himself knew, and he wasn't telling anybody.

During those years he began to take more and more interest in the estate at Hyde Park. He wanted to modernize the farm, make it a paying proposition.

"For what it costs us to drink the milk we produce here," he told his mother, "we might as well be drinking champagne!"

But his mother would have none of his "new-fangled notions." As long as she lived, she announced firmly, the farm would be operated exactly as her husband had operated it. For years she used to ride around the farm on horseback, as her husband had done, looking things over. When she could ride no longer, she drove herself in a buggy. She never changed. Until she died, in her eighties, the farm was run as James had run it.

Around the Roosevelt land there were a number of worked-out, abandoned farms. Franklin must have had to dip into his principal to do it, but the bored young New York lawyer started buying them up. To restore the soil, he planted tiny evergreens, mostly spruces, which could be obtained from the state forestry service free of charge.

Franklin Roosevelt also began to participate in civic affairs in the town of Hyde Park. He joined the volunteer fire department, attended various meetings and once casually looked into the possibility of running for town supervisor, a position his father had once held.

By 1910 Uncle Ted was out of the White House, had been on a big-game hunting trip in Africa and had made a triumphal tour of Europe. All over the world, Teddy Roosevelt received adulation akin, in a lesser degree, to that which Winston Churchill has received since World War II. A dramatic and colorful person was "T.R." Back in this country, he was becoming disillusioned with the conservative Republican he himself had picked to be his successor, William Howard Taft of Ohio. Very likely the younger Roosevelt felt as he did, although he himself had not yet made any definite move to enter politics.

Just how Franklin Roosevelt entered politics is not quite clear. One or two of his biographers say he made the first move, asking the Democratic leaders in his home county, Dutchess, about letting him run for the State Assembly. But the account given by most of them— and still told by some old-timers around Hyde Park—is that the leaders approached him. They were looking around for somebody to run for the State Senate and help fill the ticket, not an easy assignment, since the area was so overwhelmingly Republican that a Democratic candidate, they thought, wouldn't have a ghost of a chance. Their motives might have been questionable, to say the least. Here was a young man with money, who would certainly pay his own expenses and might also make a substantial contribution to the general campaign fund. Innocent though he was in the ways of politicians those days, Franklin may have suspected them.

In any event, he accepted the offer with alacrity, to the surprise of most people and to his mother's disapproval. She couldn't understand why her son would want to be involved in "messy politics." She had a lot to learn, did Sara Delano Roosevelt. His wife, who never questioned his decisions involving his career, went along and tried to encourage him, despite the fact that she knew nothing about politics and was not interested in the subject. She didn't even believe in woman suffrage those days, although her husband did. She only wanted him to be happy, and she must have realized that he was bored with the law.

Uncle Ted was pleased, but regretted that Franklin was running as a Democrat. The Republicans wanted Uncle Ted to come out against him, but this Ted refused to do. As a matter of fact, Franklin always insisted that Uncle Ted was not really a Republican at all, but a Progressive.

The Democratic candidate for the State Senate from Dutchess, Putnam, and Columbia counties was only twenty-eight years old, tall, still very slender, with the charm that up to now had been more of a hindrance than a help to him, for it somehow made people fail to take him seriously. He had begun to wear, for reading, rimless eyeglasses without bows, that he clamped on his nose. Fashions in eyeglasses changed, but he wore that kind for the rest of his life. Some people noticed he had a trick of tossing his head, in an arrogant sort of way. It may have started from lack of self-assurance.

In his first speech, he said: "I accept this nomination with absolute independence. I am pledged to no man. I am influenced by no special interests. And so I shall remain." It was exactly the kind of speech candidates generally make on such occasions. Only it happened that this particular candidate meant it.

His speeches in that campaign gave no indication that Franklin Roosevelt would some day be considered one of the finest orators this nation has ever produced. Eleanor, who dutifully went along to hear him when she could (another baby, Elliott, arrived during the campaign), worried about the long pauses that occurred sometimes as he apparently hesitated, trying to think of what he was going to say next.

Nevertheless he proceeded to put on a campaign the like of which that area had never seen before. He did not own an automobile and didn't know how to drive one, so he rented an old bright red Maxwell touring car without any top, owned and driven by a man named Hawkey, and off he went, roaring, clanking, honking all over three rural counties. He gave his driver only one order.

"Whenever we see a horse," he said, "we'll stop. I don't want to make enemies out of any farmers by frightening their horses!"

Automobiles were not common in 1910, and horses, frightened by noise, were apt to start rearing, bucking, or bolting.

Poor thing though it was, compared with today's cars, the old red Maxwell enabled him to cover a great deal more ground than he could possibly have covered with a horse and carriage. And no meeting was too small or insignificant for him to address. In fact, he made it a practice to stop and chat with individual farmers, in their barnyards. There probably wasn't a single country post office or store in the three counties that he didn't visit at least once. He didn't bother about Poughkeepsie, the only large town in the area. Poughkeepsie was Democratic anyway. He concentrated on the farmers who usually, almost to a man, voted Republican. No other candidate had ever paid much attention to them. They liked this young man, who always stopped his car so it wouldn't frighten their horses, and who obviously knew what he was talking about when he discussed farming with them. He might not be a very eloquent speaker, but what he said about the subjects in which they were most interested made sense.

When the votes were finally counted, Franklin Delano Roosevelt became a State Senator. And it was the traditionally Republican "farm vote" that did it.

10

Senator Roosevelt

Most members of the New York State Legislature, when Franklin Roosevelt went to the State Senate, left their families at home and stayed in boardinghouses in Albany, going home for week ends if they could afford it. The salary was only $1,500 a year, and, since the sessions rarely lasted more than three months, they regarded it as a part-time job, which they hoped would lead to something better.

Senator Roosevelt, however, took his position very seriously indeed. He felt that he should devote his full time to it, rented a three-story furnished house near the Capitol and moved his family to Albany.

On the day he was sworn into office, along with the other members of the Legislature, the Governor, and the rest of the state officials, the young Roosevelts (Franklin's twenty-ninth birthday was still a month away) held open house, with a professional caterer in charge. No other State Senator had ever done that before, and the party was literally mobbed, to the dismay of the caterer, who almost ran out of food.

As a new State Senator, Franklin Roosevelt unwittingly placed himself in the position he had been in when he was a new boy at Groton. He was "different." For instance, on the first few formal occasions, he appeared in morning coat, striped trousers, and top hat. He was probably the only member of the Legislature who owned such an outfit. It undoubtedly drew wisecracks from another young man, Assemblyman Alfred E. Smith, from the Lower East Side in New York. It got Franklin off to a very bad start with a youthful State Senator from New York City named Bob Wagner, whose son would some day become Mayor of the city. Eventually the three men would become good friends —but not then!

Being older and more experienced than he had been when he entered Groton, Senator Roosevelt very soon realized that his formal clothes were wrong and sent them back to Hyde Park, to be packed away in moth balls. From that time on, throughout his long political career, he shied away from formal attire and dressed that way only when it was expected of him.

There was something else about him, however, that, until his associates came to know him better, tended to set him apart and make him unpopular. This was his trick of tossing his head and seeming to look down his nose at people. That, along with his Harvard accent, caused many at first to regard him as a snob. Since he was unaware of this gesture, he did nothing about it, and the habit remained with him for the rest of his life. In later years, however, after he had demonstrated that he was by no means a snob, and that his sympathy was always with the underdog—"the forgotten man," as he said—only his most bitter enemies criticized him for it.

The young man had barely had time to cut his teeth as a senator before he became involved in one of the biggest political fights of his career, a fight that attracted the attention of the whole state and "made" him, as the politicians would say. It also drew to his side a newspaperman named Louis McHenry Howe, who was to become one of the most intimate and unselfish friends he ever had.

In 1911 United States Senators in New York were not elected by the voters, as they now are. They were elected by the State Legislature. That year a new United States Senator was to be chosen. The Democrats had won control of the Legislature, something that rarely happens in New York, so, with the Democrats in control, a Democrat would get the job.

Tammany Hall, the Democratic organization that ran the City of New York, had a candidate. Tammany Hall not only had control of New York City, but carried great weight upstate, since in the normally Republican Legislature, it presented a solid bloc of Democratic votes. Both Al Smith and Bob Wagner were Tammany men—a candidate practically had to belong to Tammany to get elected to anything in Democratic New York City. So everybody assumed that the Tammany candidate would be a "shoo-in," as the gentlemen around Albany put it.

Tammany's candidate was a man called "Blue-eyed Billy" Sheehan, a rich New York lawyer. Some of the newly elected Democratic members of the Legislature from upstate New York looked askance at "Blue-eyed Billy." Even less did they care for Charley Murphy, the Tammany chief, who was supposed to be the most powerful Democrat in the state. Tammany Hall had not helped elect them, and they didn't like political bosses. They came from districts that had supported Uncle Ted, and he fought the bosses in his own party.

Circulating among them, Senator Roosevelt, who had always admired Uncle Ted for fighting the bosses, soon found himself in a head-on collision with Charley Murphy and Tammany Hall. He had learned a good deal about organizing on the Harvard campus, and before long he had lined up twenty-one upstate Democrats, enough to prevent the election of "Blue-eyed Billy" if they stayed away from sessions at which his candidacy would come up for a vote.

Many of the newspaper correspondents didn't like Charley Murphy either and did not approve of "Blue-eyed Billy." One of them was a correspondent from a New York City paper, a little man who was a chain-smoker and was always dropping cigaret ashes on his vest. Louis McHenry Howe, after he had recovered from his shock at the top hat and the Harvard accent, was strongly attracted to the youthful Senator from Hyde Park. He admired Roosevelt's energy, his enthusiasm, liked his ideas and saw in him great promise as a political leader.

The twenty-one rebellious Democrats used to meet at the Roosevelt house, where Louis presently joined them. He was older than the Senator and knew a lot more about practical politics than he did, having had years of experience as a political writer. Although he was a practical politician, Louis Howe was also a good deal of an idealist. Before many weeks had passed, the two had formed a friendship that was to last as long as Louis lived. They were an odd pair—the reputedly wealthy, aristocratic young Harvard man and the untidy little man from Indiana, of middle-class background, who didn't care how he looked or what people thought of him.

"It won't hurt you to have a fight with Tammany," he assured Franklin Roosevelt early in the game. "You'll get a lot of publicity out of it that you could never hope to get as a freshman senator from Dutchess County. The people who voted you in will like it. It will probably re-elect you when you run again."

Louis Howe may have been more aware than Franklin Roosevelt was at that time of the growth of progressive leanings among the voters all over the country. Franklin, of course, knew that Uncle Ted was getting deeply involved in a struggle with the Republican bosses, in which he was trying to prevent the nomination for a second term of conservative President William Howard Taft. But Louis very likely was more conscious of what the struggle was doing to the Republican party. A keen observer and a man of great wisdom was Louis Howe.

"Of course," he told Franklin Roosevelt, "Tammany will never forgive you. But Tammany can't hurt you—at least not now. And a great many people outside New York City will always be in your corner."

Louis Howe undoubtedly had a hand in the strategy Senator Roosevelt and his rebels worked out. It was simple, but effective. Every day at noon, when the Legislature convened, they would report for the roll call. Then they would get up and walk out. The Democrats were helpless without those votes, and of course the Republican minority wouldn't do anything to help the Democrats.

From the Capitol they would proceed to Senator Roosevelt's house, where they would spend the rest of the day, and they would usually come back in the evening and stay until Mrs. Roosevelt would break up the session by bringing in a tray of sandwiches and coffee. They found the Roosevelts' library a much more pleasant place in which to spend an evening than their lonely rooms in the boarding-houses, and the Roosevelts were very hospitable.

The Senator's wife had only two objections. The men all smoked, mostly cigars, and the nursery, right over the library, reeked with the odor of stale cigar smoke. She finally had to move the children up to the third floor. And for once she was in complete agreement with her mother-in-law. Neither of them liked Louis Howe.

"What can you see in him?" she asked her husband.

"My dear," he replied, "that little man has given me more advice—and better advice—than anyone else I've met. He is invaluable to me. And you'd like him if you really knew him."

"Well, I wish he didn't keep dropping cigaret ashes on his vest," she sighed. "He's such an untidy little man."

In the meantime, in church one Sunday, Louis Howe remarked to his wife as the Roosevelts came in:

"You see that young man? Some day he is going to be President of the United States."

For weeks the fight dragged on, the Democrats, although they controlled the Legislature, were completely stymied by Senator Roosevelt and his rebels. A compromise had to be reached, and finally it was. Both sides dropped their candidates, and the man eventually selected, while he was a member of Tammany Hall, was acceptable to the Roosevelt group.

Neither side had really won. But, since Tammany's choice had not won, Franklin Roosevelt and his friends regarded it as a victory for their cause, and so did most people. The freshman Senator from Hyde Park had become known all over the state, and Democratic leaders outside New York were regarding him with interest.

One of them was Governor Woodrow Wilson of New Jersey, who was being widely discussed as a possible Democratic candidate for President the following year. Governor Wilson was having trouble with the Democratic bosses in his state, too, and with his progressive program, later to be known as the New Freedom, he was building up a following. Senator Roosevelt was very much interested in him, so much that in the spring of 1912, near the end of his second year in the Legislature, he betook himself to New Jersey to see the Governor.

Woodrow Wilson, austere, presenting a rather cold, aloof

exterior, was not an easy man to get to know, but he apparently warmed up to the youthful Senator from New York. They met in Governor Wilson's home in Princeton —he had been first a professor and then president of the university before he became Governor. They talked so long that Senator Roosevelt missed the last train from nearby Princeton Junction that would have taken him to New York, and had to go to Trenton, where he could catch a later train to New York.

Franklin Roosevelt went home and immediately began organizing Democrats-for-Wilson clubs.

11

"Big Navy" Man

Although he had obviously liked him on their first meeting and would always admire him for his progressive ideas, Franklin Roosevelt never had for Woodrow Wilson the hero worship that he had had for Theodore Roosevelt.

For one thing Franklin Roosevelt was more mature, although he was still only thirty, young for a successful politician, when he met Wilson. Also, he later became very critical of President Wilson for his reluctance to take the United States into World War I on the side of the Allies, though thereafter he made up for it by a loyalty to Wilson and his League of Nations that almost ended his own political career.

He was still a Wilson enthusiast when the Democratic national convention met in Baltimore in the summer of 1912 to select a candidate for President. The two leading candidates for the nomination were Woodrow Wilson and Champ Clark of Missouri, Speaker of the House of Representatives. William Jennings Bryan, who had twice been the party's unsuccessful candidate for President, ran third. Wilson led at the start, but on every vote taken in the convention, Champ Clark gained on him, until it looked as if he would win.

Then the bright young Senator from New York had an idea. He rounded up enough Wilson supporters to pack the galleries, somehow managed to get hold of enough Champ Clark buttons for all of them, so that they could get in unchallenged, and waited for the next ballot. As it started and more delegates began to switch from Wilson to Clark, the men in the galleries ripped off their Champ Clark buttons and began yelling: "We want WILSON! We want WILSON! WILSON! WILSON! WILSON!" At the same time down on the convention floor the Wilson supporters started a parade.

At that point William Jennings Bryan stepped to the front of the platform, withdrew from the race and turned the votes pledged to him over to Wilson, who thereby won the nomination.

Wilson was elected President in the fall largely because of Theodore Roosevelt. After trying unsuccessfully to prevent the nomination of President Taft for a second term, Uncle Ted became a candidate himself, on the Bull Moose ticket. This so badly split the Republican vote that Wilson was elected.

Franklin Roosevelt, himself a candidate for re-election to the New York State Senate, was unable to campaign for anyone that fall. In the Roosevelt town house in New York City, he and his wife were both down with typhoid fever. He had the worse attack and was seriously ill. Mamá, to her infinite satisfaction, kept the children, Anna, Jimmy, and Elliott, at Hyde Park and ran both households. Louis Howe, who had left his newspaper job to handle publicity for the Democrats-for-Wilson clubs, ran his friend's campaign. He did it so skillfully that Franklin Roosevelt was re-elected without making a single speech or a single public appearance. Of course, as the political writers observed, it was "a Democratic year," thanks to the split in the Republican party. But Roosevelt needed Howe—and Howe was there.

It was inevitable that President Wilson, following his inauguration, should reward William Jennings Bryan and Franklin D. Roosevelt, the two men who had played so important a part in his winning the nomination in Baltimore. William Jennings Bryan became Secretary of State, and Franklin D. Roosevelt was appointed Assistant Secretary of the Navy. In the selection of Roosevelt for the navy post, Wilson is supposed to have followed the suggestion of his Secretary of the Navy, wise old Josephus Daniels of North Carolina, long-time friend of Bryan. Daniels had met Roosevelt in Baltimore and liked his ingenuity and his youthful exuberance. Within hours after he had been offered the job, Franklin Roosevelt had resigned from the New York State Senate and was getting ready to move his family to Washington. He took Louis Howe along, as his executive assistant.

They made an odd pair, Daniels, the Secretary of the Navy, who looked like a country editor in his rumpled suit, black string tie, and dusty, square-toed shoes, and the handsome, well-dressed young aristocrat from New York, who was to serve under him. And their ideas about the Navy certainly did not jibe!

Franklin Roosevelt, who knew more about the Navy than either the President or the Secretary did, was dismayed at what he found. Uncle Ted had built up a strong Navy while he was President—so strong that once, when the German Kaiser tried to step into South America in violation of our Monroe Doctrine, he merely sent "the Great White Fleet," as the newspapers called it, down there, and the Kaiser withdrew. But under Taft, the Navy had received little attention, practically no funds, and had gone downhill. Many of the ships were now old and obsolete, many needed to go into dry dock for repairs and remodeling, and there were shortages in everything—supplies, including guns and ammunition, docks and fueling stations.

World War I was a little more than a year away when Roosevelt took office. The history he had learned at Harvard, his knowledge of world affairs and his distrust of the German Kaiser made him uneasy. He immediately started out to build up the Navy, so that, as he said, it would be "ready for any emergency." He found himself butting his head against a stone wall.

Secretary Daniels also thought we needed a better Navy. But to do so, it was up to him to get the money from Congress. And he was wise in the ways of Congress—much wiser than either Roosevelt or Howe at that stage. Congress could never be driven or forced by the executive branch of the Government. It had to be coaxed, and it took time.

There were some things about the Navy that Secretary Daniels did not like. He was inclined to regard the admirals, in their stiff white summer uniforms with yards of gold braid on them, as a bunch of snobs, and he actually issued orders that in some instances officers and enlisted men share the same quarters. Naturally the admirals were furious, and they took their troubles to the Assistant Secretary. Democratic though he was at heart, Franklin Roosevelt had great respect for Navy traditions. He couldn't help sympathizing with the admirals. He knew better than Daniels did how necessary it was to maintain tradition and strict discipline in the Navy.

In the summer of 1914, the war in Europe finally broke out. The Assistant Secretary assumed that this country would immediately start to build up its Navy, but he was doomed to nearly three years of frustration, bitter disappointment and inner fury. Still the Secretary cautioned patience, gently nudging Congress, but getting nowhere, and the President and the Secretary of State, adhering to our traditional refusal to become involved in European affairs, urged "watchful waiting." The public was on their side. The American people never want to go to war—as Franklin Roosevelt himself was to find out some thirty years later!

Franklin Roosevelt has been severely criticized for some of the things he did during that period. It has been said that he was disloyal to Secretary Daniels and to President Wilson himself. On one or two occasions he made speeches criticizing the attitude of the Administration. Many people thought he was much too intimate, socially, with the British and French ambassadors, who naturally wanted the United States to get into the war and help the Allies. It was rumored that a coolness had grown up between the Secretary and his assistant. But there is no record that either the Secretary or the President tried to slap the young man down. Daniels maintained a patient, fatherly attitude toward him, which Roosevelt in time would understand and for which he would always be grateful.

Finally it happened, as Franklin Roosevelt had thought it inevitably must. On an April evening in 1917, following the sinking by a German submarine of the ocean liner *Lusitania,* Woodrow Wilson, with a heavy heart, went up to the Capitol and delivered one of the most eloquent speeches of his career, asking Congress to declare war on Germany. And William Jennings Bryan resigned as Secretary of State. His old friend, Josephus Daniels, must have sympathized with him—it was for Bryan the end of a long political career. But it never occurred to Daniels to quit. Now he would be in a position to give effective backing to his impetuous, but capable, Assistant Secretary.

The floodgates were opened, money was available at last, and Franklin Roosevelt had a free hand. He moved with lightning speed and started building, organizing and buying up everything in sight. So much so that, a few months after we entered the war, President Wilson sent for him and said, with dry humor: "Mr. Secretary, you seem to have cornered the market on all supplies needed for both branches of the service. I'm sorry, but you'll have to divide up with the Army."

During the early weeks after we got into the war, Franklin Roosevelt found himself in a sad situation. Uncle Ted, whom he had worshiped as a boy and for whom he had always had the greatest affection and admiration, wanted to enlist an army division of volunteers and lead it to Europe, duplicating on a larger scale his feat in the Spanish-American War. President Wilson, however, was cool to the idea from the start. Uncle Ted was no longer a young man, and the President may have had doubts as to how he would get on with the man chosen to lead the American Expeditionary Force to France, General "Black Jack" Pershing.

Uncle Ted came down to Washington and asked Franklin to help him. Franklin tried, but to no avail. President Wilson finally said no. This may have been the last time the two Roosevelts saw each other. Theodore Roosevelt died in New York a few weeks after the end of the war. His favorite niece, Eleanor, and her husband were out of the country when it happened.

Once he had things moving to his satisfaction, the Assistant Secretary of the Navy tried to resign and get into uniform. He recalled what his father had told him when he was a boy—that if we ever got into another war, he should have no difficulty getting a commission in the Navy. Here was his chance. All his life he had wanted some day to wear the Navy blue, but when he proposed it to his chief and to the President, they turned him down. Obstreperous though he had been in the past, the two older men understood him and appreciated his ability. He was too valuable where he was, they told him. It was a high compliment, but it didn't comfort Roosevelt much.

Valuable he certainly was. His most important contribution—in addition to building up the Navy to war strength in an unbelievably short time—came from his willingness to listen to a new idea. One day an inventor came to him with a plan for an electrical submarine trap, a kind of net, wired with electricity, that could be stretched across the English Channel or anywhere else, to bottle up the German submarines, which were constantly sinking Allied ships. The American admirals couldn't see anything in it, but the Assistant Secretary could, and he kept pushing it until the British Navy took it up. The net was finally stretched across a passage in the North Sea, through which German submarines would pass, heading for the English Channel and the Atlantic Ocean. It was credited with having destroyed more than 200 German submarines and having thereby helped end the war.

Life for the Roosevelts during the Washington years was neither easy nor tranquil. More children came. In the late summer of 1914 another boy, whom they named Franklin Delano Roosevelt, Jr., arrived. There had been an earlier Franklin, Jr., born between Jimmy and Elliott, but he died when he was only a few months old. And in 1916 the last baby, John Aspinwall Roosevelt, arrived and was named after his father's Uncle John. As Assistant Secretary of the Navy, Franklin Roosevelt received only $5,000 a year. That, added to their combined incomes, was not enough. The older children were in school, expensive schools, considered proper for descendants of the Delanos and the Roosevelts. There were the usual childhood illnesses. And it cost money to move in the social circle in which the Roosevelts were expected to move. Mamá frequently had to come to the rescue, at the same time keeping a tight hold on her "children" and her grandchildren. Eleanor Roosevelt, busy with war work, was becoming more mature and more and more restless under her mother-in-law's domination.

In the summer of 1918, the Assistant Secretary finally had a chance to go overseas on an inspection trip. He had from President Wilson a promise that, on his return, he could resign and go into uniform. It was a successful trip. He went everywhere. He even put on khaki and went up into the front-line trenches. But on the way home he became ill with double pneumonia and had to be carried off the ship on a stretcher, a very sick man. By the time he had recovered, it was too late for him to get his Navy commission. The Armistice was only a few days away.

Toward the end of his life, some people wondered why Franklin Roosevelt in cold weather always wore a big, heavy, dark blue cape. It was the kind of cape Navy officers used to wear with their dress uniforms. As Commander in Chief of the Armed Forces, he was entitled to wear it if he desired.

That heavy, rather awkward cape was as close as Franklin Roosevelt ever came to wearing what all his life he had wanted to wear—the uniform of an officer in the United States Navy.

12

Unsuccessful Politician

On January 1, 1919, Assistant Secretary of the Navy and Mrs. Franklin D. Roosevelt sailed for Europe on the liner *George Washington*. World War I had ended, and it was Roosevelt's job to wind up Navy business with our allies. With the exception of Mrs. Wilson, who would presently accompany the President to the Peace Conference in Paris, government officials were not permitted to take their wives with them overseas at that time. The Armistice was only a few weeks old, and conditions in Europe were chaotic. In the case of Mrs. Roosevelt, however, an exception was made, for her husband was still weak from his siege with double pneumonia following which he had contracted influenza when it swept the country in the fall of 1918.

Both Franklin Roosevelt and his wife wanted to see as much of the devastation as they could, and they managed to see a great deal, to the disapproval of the military leaders. Mrs. Roosevelt, suffering from pleurisy, accompanied her husband, still weak from his illness, on a tour of the trenches and the battlefields.

"You can't take Mrs. Roosevelt up to the front lines," a British officer, in command in one sector, said firmly.

"But I already have," her husband replied cheerfully.

What they saw on that tour—the ravaged villages and farms, the filthy trenches overrun with rats, the rows and rows of little white crosses over hastily dug graves—made them both fighters for peace for the rest of their lives. Although she had worked hard for the Red Cross in the little tin shack that served as a canteen for the troops passing through Union Station in Washington in 1917 and 1918, Eleanor Roosevelt had little knowledge of world politics and had not shown much interest in it up to that time. She still took no part in public affairs for several years after the trip, but it changed her attitude a great deal. It also changed the thinking of her husband, "the big Navy man," who heretofore had been thoroughly nationalistic. For the rest of his life, he would be saying: *"I hate war."*

Since Franklin Roosevelt was not a member of the American delegation, they watched the Peace Conference and the development of President Wilson's idea, the League of Nations, which was designed to end all wars, from the side lines. Franklin Roosevelt did not see a copy of the Covenant of the League until he and his wife were on a train bound from Paris to Brest on their way home, when a newspaperman showed it to him.

After weeks of wrangling and debate, the Allies had signed the Peace Treaty and had adopted the Covenant of the League of Nations by the time President and Mrs. Wilson sailed for home on the *George Washington*. Aboard also were the Roosevelts, and Franklin Roosevelt was immensely pleased and proud when one day President Wilson sent for him and spent an hour talking with him about the League. The President had the Covenant in his pocket, the rest of the world had accepted it, but the United States Senate would have to ratify it before this nation could join the League. That President Wilson may have been tormented by doubt even then might be surmised from a remark he made while he and Mrs. Wilson were entertaining the Roosevelts at lunch one day on the ship.

"The United States must go in or it will break the heart of the world," President Wilson said earnestly. Neither Franklin nor Eleanor Roosevelt ever forgot that remark.

Back in this country, Roosevelt and Louis Howe went about the job of bringing the Navy back to a peace-time basis. Installations had to be dismantled, surplus property disposed of and some of the ships "put in moth balls," as the Navy men expressed it.

During the years while the Assistant Secretary was building up the Navy, Louis Howe had done a great deal of excellent work, for which he never got much credit. One of his jobs was to handle labor problems in the shipyards. During that period, both he and Roosevelt had their first real contact with labor. They were shocked at the low wages paid the men in the shipyards and succeeded in getting them raised. This was no small achievement, since the men were not organized powerfully as they are now. Howe's competence was appreciated in some quarters. In 1916, after he had visited the New Orleans Navy yard, the naval constructor there wrote the Assistant Secretary:

"It is a source of wonder to me how a man not connected with the Naval service can have obtained in three years the detailed knowledge of the situation that is possessed by Mr. Howe."

By the time he went to Washington, Franklin Roosevelt had found his career. It would be politics. With Louis Howe at his elbow, it could hardly have been otherwise, even if Roosevelt himself had not been interested. And interested he certainly was. As for Louis, he had long since made up his mind that his young political protégé would some day be President of the United States. An astute, resourceful, and determined man was Mr. Howe.

Naturally they turned their attention to New York State. Although he was Assistant Secretary of the Navy, Franklin Roosevelt was relatively unknown outside his own state. Charley Murphy, the Tammany leader, had never forgiven him for the fight in the State Senate over "Blue-eyed Billy" Sheehan, and Roosevelt had little regard for Murphy and his bossism. With some private encouragement from President Wilson, Franklin Roosevelt tried to organize upstate progressives into a Democratic opposition to Tammany. He had little success. Uncle Ted was a progressive, too, and since most of Franklin's upstate friends had always in the past been Republicans, they naturally leaned toward a Republican, rather than a Democratic, progressive.

In the meantime, Tammany was in trouble. In 1912 the organization had helped elect a Democratic governor, "Plain Bill" Sulzer, who did not have a very good reputation. Immediately after his inauguration, Sulzer turned against Tammany, whereupon the infuriated Tammany leaders started impeachment proceedings, charging that he had speculated in the stock market with campaign funds. The Legislature impeached Sulzer, and he was thrown out of office. So badly shattered was the party that its state chairman said gloomily that he did not see how a Democrat could be elected to anything in New York State. That year, 1913, the Democrats lost in practically all of the municipal elections. They couldn't even carry New York City. John Purroy Mitchel, an independent, was elected Mayor.

Another state election was coming up in 1914, and some of the newspapers started booming Roosevelt for Governor or United States Senator. The law had been changed so that United States Senators were elected by the voters, after first running in a primary election. Young Roosevelt, still in his early thirties, ambitious and frustrated in his effort to build up the Navy, couldn't help being flattered and tempted. More energetically than ever, he went to work trying to organize a progressive Democratic party in up-state New York. In his enthusiasm, he got a bit out of bounds and was coldly cautioned by President Wilson, who wrote him:

"In my judgement it would be best if members of the administration should use as much influence as possible but say as little as possible in the politics of their several states."

In the next sentence he referred specifically to New York State.

But as the 1914 September primaries approached, the pressure on the Assistant Secretary increased. Finally on August 13, after having said repeatedly that he would not be a candidate, he suddenly announced that he would run for the United States Senate. Had Louis Howe been around, he might not have done it, but Louis Howe was away on a vacation. That night he sent Louis a telegram saying: "My senses have not yet left me."

He had made a bad mistake, for presently he found himself running in the primary against one of the most highly respected men in the Wilson administration, James W. Gerard, ambassador to Germany. Wilson, of course, remained neutral, while Roosevelt stumped the state. Gerard could not leave his post in Berlin to campaign. World War I had started, and he was busy getting Americans out of Germany. None the less, in the primary he beat Roosevelt, two-to-one outside New York City, four-to-one in the city. His victory did not mean much, however, for in the final election he was beaten by a Republican, James W. Wadsworth. 1914 was not a Democratic year.

After his defeat in the primary, Franklin Roosevelt devoted less time to politics, concentrating his attention on the Navy. But Louis Howe continued a practice he had begun while his friend was in the State Senate. He kept a constant stream of letters, over Roosevelt's signature, flowing into New York State. In 1918, Tammany, desperately looking for a candidate who might win, approached Roosevelt with an offer to back him for Governor. But Roosevelt, anxious to get into a Navy uniform, was not interested.

By 1920, the League of Nations had run into implacable opposition in the United States Senate, opposition led by a group of Republican Senators headed by Senator Henry Cabot Lodge of Massachusetts, whom President Wilson had failed to take into his confidence. The President himself, exhausted, had gone on a tour of the country, trying to win support from the people, had collapsed while on the trip, and would spend the rest of his life a broken, enfeebled old man. The American people, tired of the war, had little interest in the League. The Senate eventually failed to ratify the Covenant, and the United States remained out of the League of Nations.

The Democratic national convention that year was held in San Francisco. Franklin Roosevelt went out alone—his wife spent the summer with "the chicks," as he called his children, at Campobello. The situation for the Democrats looked so hopeless that they had a hard time finding a candidate for President. They finally settled on James M. Cox, former Governor of Ohio, who was relatively unknown. Franklin Roosevelt was standing out in the corridor, talking with a friend, when someone came running out and announced: "You're being nominated for Vice-President!" To which Roosevelt is said to have replied: "Quit kidding me!"

But he *was* nominated, along with Cox. Shortly thereafter the two men went to the White House to see President Wilson. Franklin Roosevelt still regarded the League as the world's best hope for peace, and he imparted some of his feeling to his running mate. They found President Wilson sitting in a wheel chair on the South Veranda, a shawl draped over his paralyzed left arm. His voice was weak as he thanked them for coming, but some of the old fire came back as Cox said: "Mr. President, we are going to be a million per cent for you and your administration, and that means the League of Nations." Woodrow Wilson's voice was stronger, his expression earnest as he replied: "Thank you. I am very grateful."

The exuberant Republicans, confident of victory, had selected their candidate in "a smoke-filled room"—meaning a private conference of the bosses—after a heated battle among several contenders. The man they chose was United States Senator Warren G. Harding of Ohio, a politician who had done little to distinguish himself.

Cox and Roosevelt, who must have realized from the start that they were fighting a losing battle, vigorously went to work. In that campaign Roosevelt was accompanied by his wife, whose heart was in the fight he was making, although she was still too shy to do any speaking, and, of course, by Louis Howe. To Howe, it must have looked hopeless, too, but he was convinced that Roosevelt was doing the right thing, the only thing he could do. On one trip during that campaign, Franklin Roosevelt covered twenty states in eighteen days, averaging seven speeches a day. He was becoming an excellent speaker. And his wife, for the first time, began to understand and to appreciate Louis Howe.

Harding did not travel much. He just sat on his front porch in Marion, Ohio, and talked about getting the country "back to normalcy." He couldn't have had a better campaign slogan. It was exactly what the American people wanted to hear, and all the politicians knew it. Things got so bad that Democratic candidates for Congress and

88

state offices refused even to mention the League in their speeches. Still Cox and Roosevelt battled on—hopelessly, tirelessly, gallantly. Nobody was surprised on Election Day, when the Democrats were swamped. Warren Harding was elected President by a big majority.

Franklin D. Roosevelt had suffered his second defeat at the polls. Since a man who runs for Vice-President and loses is usually finished, Franklin Roosevelt's political future did not look very bright to anyone—except Louis Howe.

13

"A Babies' Disease?"

In November, 1920, right after the smash-
ing Republican victory, Franklin Roosevelt resigned as Assistant Secretary of the Navy and
moved his family back to their town house in
New York.

He needed a job. In Washington he had always run a
little behind financially, even with his mother's help. From
now on their expenses would increase. Anna was in finishing school, Jimmy was at Groton, Elliott and Franklin, Jr.,
were enrolled in a private day school which was by no
means cheap, and John, under five, still had a nursery governess. And whether they wanted it or not, the family had
to live according to standards set, and partly maintained,
by Mamá. They must have a cook, second maid, laundress,
butler, and chauffeur. They must do a great deal of entertaining on the Delano-Roosevelt level. Eleanor Roosevelt
was supposed to be "the Mistress," not a housekeeper. She
knew little about housekeeping anyway and could not cook
a meal. In a few weeks—on January 30, 1921—her husband would be thirty-nine years old.

He found a job without difficulty, thanks to his friend,
Van Lear Black, a wealthy Baltimore industrialist, who

hired him to become vice-president in charge of the New York office of the Fidelity and Deposit Company of Maryland, at a salary of $25,000 a year. He also entered a law firm with his friends Grenville T. Emmet and Langdon P. Marvin. He spent mornings at his job down near Wall Street, and afternoons in his law office. The legal profession still did not interest him much, but he needed the money.

For a man who had been defeated in a campaign for the vice-presidency and was therefore no longer an important political figure, the demands on his time, for nonpaying jobs, were astonishing. He was made an overseer of Harvard University, a director of the Seamen's Church Institute, president of the Navy Club, chairman of the $2,000,000 fund drive for the Lighthouse for the Blind, chairman of the Greater New York Committee of the Boy Scouts of America, a member of the Near East Relief Committee, the Council of the American Geographic Society, and the executive committee of the American Civic Federation. He also led in establishing the Woodrow Wilson Foundation. He had made an excellent reputation for himself as a speaker during the campaign and was constantly in demand for nonpolitical speeches. Although he had not lost interest, he did little in politics. But Louis Howe, who had remained behind in Washington to wind up details in turning the Navy Department over to the Republicans, kept a sensitive finger on the political pulse. He could not have helped doing it had he tried. Politics came as naturally to him as eating (he was a great epicure) or smoking! And he was still firmly convinced that some day Franklin D. Roosevelt would be President of the United States.

Franklin Roosevelt's mother spent the summer of 1921 in Europe. His wife took the children, a retinue of servants, a French-speaking governess—Mamá insisted that the children learn to speak fluent French—and two dogs up to Campobello. Her husband stayed in New York working most of the summer. In early August, Van Lear Black took him up to Campobello on his yacht. The summer heat in New York had been bad, and among children there was a good deal of infantile paralysis. Franklin Roosevelt took note of it, and was very glad that his "chicks" were safe up at "Campo," as the family called their summer home.

Mrs. Roosevelt thought her husband looked thin and tired when he arrived. He admitted that he felt "a bit listless," but he entered immediately upon a strenuous vacation program. He went fishing with Van Lear Black and fell into the icy water of the Bay of Fundy. "I thought I never would get warm again," he told his wife that evening. Van Lear Black left soon after, and Roosevelt planned to take his children on a camping trip. They had a house guest, Louis Howe's little boy Hartley, who, with his mother, had come up for a visit. Louis, now finished with the Navy, was to arrive in a few days for a vacation before starting on a new job.

The afternoon before the camping trip was supposed to start, Franklin Roosevelt took the children for a sail on their new boat, the *Vireo*. They were on their way home when they saw a forest fire burning on one of the islands. They immediately went ashore, Roosevelt cut off some pine branches, and they started beating out the flames. It took a long time, for the fire had got a good start, and when they finally finished they were all black with smoke and dirt, their clothes were burned with sparks and their eyes were red and smarting from the smoke.

"How about a swim?" the children's father suggested as they tied up at their home dock. And they all raced across the island to the little lake, where the water was comparatively warm.

"Let's take a dip in the bay," Elliott suggested.

"Well, only for a few minutes," his father said. "That water is darned cold!"

After their dip in the bay, they dogtrotted home. As he crossed the veranda, Franklin Roosevelt noticed on a table a pile of mail which had been brought over from the mainland that afternoon. There were several letters for him, and he sat down in his wet bathing suit to read them and to glance through the papers.

"I felt terribly tired," he recalled later. "The dip in the bay hadn't had the bracing effect that it usually had."

As he was getting dressed, he felt a pain in his back. He went down to dinner, but the pain kept getting worse, and he finally said he thought he was having an attack of lumbago, excused himself, and went upstairs to bed.

When he got up the following morning he noticed that his left leg didn't want to work. "It's probably some muscular thing," he told himself, and he stamped hard several times on his left foot, shook himself, shaved, and started to get dressed. But the left leg kept getting weaker, and before he had finished dressing he felt so ill that he went back to bed. When Anna brought up his breakfast on a tray, he managed to laugh a little and joke with her. "It isn't anything," he assured her. "Just a cold." But his wife came in with a thermometer a few minutes later, took his temperature, and sent their launch over to the mainland to get Dr. E. H. Bennett, who was their family physician when they were at Campobello.

"He has a temperature of 102°," she announced with a worried frown as the doctor came in.

In spite of the trouble with the leg, Dr. Bennett agreed with the patient that it was "just a bad cold." Mrs. Roosevelt was so concerned that she sent the children off on their camping trip with a friend so the house would be quiet.

By evening, her husband's right leg was bothering him, too, and by the next morning, August 12, he could not stand up. By that evening, he could not move his legs at all. They were numb, yet hurt badly if anyone touched them. He seemed to be partly paralyzed from the chest down, and when he tried to write a check, his hand could not hold the pen.

"It's something much more serious than a cold," Dr. Bennett said when he came the next morning. "It's some kind of paralysis. We'd better call in someone who knows more about it than I do."

In the meantime Louis Howe had arrived, and he started looking for a specialist. Campobello Island is a remote place; it was hard to find anyone. He finally located a famous specialist who was spending his vacation at Bar Harbor, Maine. After examining the patient, the specialist diagnosed the trouble as a blood clot in the lower spinal cord, prescribed heavy massage, predicted that he would eventually recover and went away. Later he sent a bill for $600.

At Campobello it was impossible to get a trained nurse, let alone anyone who knew how to give the kind of massage the doctor had ordered, so Mrs. Roosevelt and Louis Howe did the best they could. By this time, Franklin Roosevelt's legs had become so sensitive that he could hardly keep from screaming if anyone touched the sheet on his bed. And he was completely paralyzed from the chest down.

"How he ever endured that massage, I'll never know," his wife said later. "Louis and I were clumsy at it, I know, and probably hurt him more than a professional would, but he gritted his teeth and bore it. Never once did he let out a cry or a moan. And the bad thing about it was that we were doing exactly the wrong thing."

After a couple of days, with no sign of improvement,

94

Eleanor Roosevelt telephoned her husband's uncle, Frederic A. Delano, in New York. After consulting several specialists, "Uncle Fred" sent Dr. Robert W. Lovett of Boston to Campobello. Dr. Lovett was a specialist in infantile paralysis, and he recognized the disease at once.

"Infantile paralysis?" Franklin Roosevelt exclaimed and added impatiently: "It *can't* be! That's a babies' disease. I'm thirty-nine years old!"

"I'm sorry, Mr. Roosevelt," Dr. Lovett replied, "but it is."

He was a little reassuring, however, as he said it was a mild case and predicted that the patient would ultimately recover completely.

The days dragged by. After a week, Franklin Roosevelt's temperature went down to normal, and he began to regain the use of his arms and hands, but the rest of his body, from the chest down, was still paralyzed. He could not sit up. Since he was completely helpless and could not be left alone, Mrs. Roosevelt had a bed made up on the window seat in his bedroom and slept there—fitfully. Night and day, she was always at his bedside.

The boy who had learned at Groton never to whine or whimper, had grown into a man who could endure weeks and months of almost unbelievable physical torture without ever complaining. Naturally the children were frightened. They were not allowed to go into their father's room, and their mother did everything she could to keep them playing outdoors. But several times a day one or more of them would stand in the doorway, looking at first as though they were about to cry. Then their father would think of something funny to say. He was always cheerful in their presence, no matter how much pain he was suffering.

His own mental anguish he described years later to an old friend. "I thought God had forsaken me," he said. "I could not see what good could come out of it, although I tried hard to think so." But he never said a word about it to his wife, or to Louis Howe. His mother had hurried home from Europe and arrived at Campobello on September 1. He greeted her: "Well, I am glad you are back, Mummy. I got up this party for you." Dr. Bennett came in, and a few minutes later she heard them laughing in her son's room, Franklin, his wife, and the doctor.

Louis Howe did not lose hope. So far as he was concerned, Franklin Roosevelt's career was not ended, no matter how badly the disease might cripple him. Some day Franklin D. Roosevelt would be President of the United States. Louis Howe would not consider the possibility of defeat—even as his candidate lay flat on his back, trying for hours to wiggle one big toe.

14 | Not Surrender— Readjustment

Lying in bed at Campobello in the late summer of 1921, unable to move his legs or sit up, suffering excruciating pain most of the time, Franklin Roosevelt had to make a decision. It was forced upon him by his adoring, possessive mother, who thought she knew more than the doctors did, had convinced herself that he was going to be an invalid for the rest of his life and was determined to take him back to Hyde Park and take care of him.

No one knew how fully aware he was of the seriousness of his illness, although it may be assumed that he did not accept his mother's opinion. Dr. Lovett, in his presence at least, had been reassuring. He had said it was a mild case of infantile paralysis and had predicted complete recovery. Roosevelt may have simply taken his word for it, as anyone under the circumstances would have wanted to do. If he had any doubts, he revealed them to no one. Following his schoolboy habit, he kept his own counsel.

For the immediate future, two courses lay open for him. He could accede to his mother's wish, drop all his business, civic, and political connections, retire to Hyde Park and become a permanent invalid. Or he could return to New

York City, live as active a life as possible and fight for complete recovery. His decision, as stated by Frank Freidel, one of the most reliable of his biographers, was to meet the situation "not with surrender but with readjustment."

He made his choice quickly, and he had no need to announce it. His actions indicated it. Ten days after he became paralyzed, while his right hand was so weak that he could not hold a pen to sign his name, he agreed to serve on an endowment fund committee for Vassar College, and a few days later he accepted an appointment to the executive committee of the New York Democratic State Committee. From that time on, for seven long years while he fought gamely, but without success, to regain the use of his legs, he was never out of touch with business, politics, or civic affairs.

His mother refused to take his decision seriously. To her it was incomprehensible that her son and heir should be unwilling to move his family to Hyde Park and let her support them—and dominate them. What followed would inevitably have occurred sometime. Franklin Roosevelt's wife had already begun to draw away from the stuffy, restricted life her mother-in-law considered suitable for her. It had started in Washington, where she had worked twelve hours a day as a volunteer in a Red Cross canteen. During the preceding winter she had taken cooking lessons, studied shorthand and typing, and had become active in the League of Women Voters. She was no longer the timid, docile daughter-in-law she had once been. Now the two women faced each other in a conflict that would continue for months and years. For Eleanor Roosevelt was just as determined that her husband should *not* become a permanent invalid as his mother was that he *should*.

She had from the beginning one ally, Louis Howe. Louis was of course anathema to Sara Roosevelt, as he always would be. But Eleanor Roosevelt, who had begun to understand and like the raspy, untidy little man while her husband was running for Vice-President, now found in him a tremendous source of strength and hope. Howe dropped all his personal plans to remain at Franklin Roosevelt's side for the rest of his own life. It was a sacrifice Eleanor Roosevelt felt that neither she nor her husband could ever fully repay.

The days for Louis Howe preceding the removal of Franklin Roosevelt to a hospital in New York were arduous and trying. During the years, he had built up a reputation for always being truthful to the press. Now he had to conceal the fact that Roosevelt was as ill as he really was. If he did not recover quickly, the truth must be admitted to the public slowly and carefully, with each statement showing some improvement. He was aided somewhat by the remoteness of Campobello Island, but every few days a reporter for one of the press associations would hire a launch and go over to the island, where Louis would meet him on the dock, smoking and wheezing—he had asthma from too many cigarets—and assure him that the patient was improving every day, although perhaps he had been sicker than they had thought at first, and that he would soon be up and around as usual.

The removal of Franklin Roosevelt from Campobello Island on September 13 to a private car in the railroad yards at Eastport, Maine, required some adroit planning on the part of Howe. The patient had to be moved on a stretcher because he still could not sit up without support, although he had recovered some use of his hands and arms. He was taken in an open launch to the mainland, carried up a steep incline, through the railroad yards and finally shoved through an open window into the private car. Howe was determined that the press and public must not see Roosevelt in that condition. Louis managed to prevent it by circulating a rumor that Roosevelt would arrive at a dock on the opposite side of the town. By the time the reporters and the crowd caught up with him, Franklin Roosevelt, fully dressed, was sitting propped up against some pillows in his drawing room jauntily smoking a cigaret. Of the pain and exhaustion the trip must have cost him he gave no indication, as he laughed and joked with his well-wishers.

The public never knew that Franklin Roosevelt had infantile paralysis until after he had entered Presbyterian Hospital, in New York City. Then Louis Howe gave out a carefully worded statement saying that he had poliomyelitis and had lost the use of his legs *below the knees*. Dr. George Draper, who had been one of his schoolmates at Groton, now became Roosevelt's physician, and Howe's statement quoted him as saying, "He will not be crippled." (At that very moment Franklin Roosevelt was still paralyzed from the chest down except for partial use of his hands and arms, and Dr. Draper wrote Dr. Lovett that he doubted that he would ever be able to sit up again.)

Dr. Draper had a reason, however, for making that optimistic statement. It was extremely important that his patient's morale be kept high. For that reason he did not examine Roosevelt's hands and arms, for Roosevelt insisted that they were getting stronger every day, and the doctor did not want to discourage him. So well did Louis Howe and Dr. Draper succeed with their statement that only a few days after he entered the hospital Franklin Roosevelt received a letter from Herbert Pell of the Democratic State Committee asking him to attend a meeting. Louis scrawled on the margin, before he turned the letter over to Roosevelt: "Mr. Pell had better wake up and hear the birdies!"

With the addition of Dr. Draper, Franklin Roosevelt

at that point had gathered around him a devoted group of three, who would fight with every resource at their command his mother's fierce determination to dominate him. He needed their support, and he got it. In addition to his wife, Louis Howe, and Dr. Draper, there was a fourth member. She was Marguerite LeHand, his secretary. She, like Louis, would spend the rest of her life at his elbow, a completely loyal and invaluable assistant. Louis settled his wife, his daughter and son in an apartment in Poughkeepsie and moved in with the Roosevelts. Van Lear Black gave him a job as Roosevelt's executive assistant. Later Miss LeHand would also become part of the household. The family called her "Missy." They all did everything they could to keep up Roosevelt's morale, and Louis and Missy from the beginning worked unceasingly to maintain his contacts with the outside world. From the time Roosevelt left the hospital on October 28, a steady stream of letters flowed out of his home on 65th Street. By that time, Roosevelt was able to sign them, but Louis and Missy did the work.

That winter in the Roosevelt town house was one that none of those who lived through it liked to remember. As the weeks went by the bitterness of Sara Roosevelt toward her daughter-in-law grew more and more intense. It was also directed to some extent toward Louis Howe and Dr. Draper, but most of it was centered on her son's wife. It became so bad that she even tried to turn Anna against her mother.

The house was badly overcrowded after they brought the patient home from the hospital. Anna had to give up her room and bath to Louis Howe and sleep up on the fourth floor. Anna was still an adolescent and needed much more attention from her father and mother than either of them could give her at that time. She felt neglected and resentful over having to give up her room to Louis,

101

whose constant presence was as important to her father as the care Dr. Draper was giving him. But Anna did not understand that, she did not like Louis (none of the children did) and her grandmother played on her resentment and had her convinced that her mother did not really love her. Room also had to be made for a trained nurse, so Anna's mother slept on a cot in the boys' room. But nobody paid any attention to that, for she never complained.

The situation came to a head when Eleanor Roosevelt burst into tears one afternoon while she was reading aloud to Franklin, Jr., and Johnny. She found a room temporarily empty, locked herself in, and cried for hours. It was the only time she ever broke down. A day or so later, she managed to have a long, quiet talk with her daughter, explained why Louis Howe was so necessary to her father, and as a result "Granny's" influence on the child was considerably diminished.

Slowly and surely Eleanor Roosevelt was winning the battle, but her mother-in-law fought every inch of the way. Sara Roosevelt was losing something that meant more to her than anything else in life, the power to direct the lives of her son and his wife. Deep down she must have known she was losing, but she would not admit it, even to herself. There was evidence that she never really forgave her daughter-in-law, for, to the end of her life, she would frequently address her with sugar-coated barbs. But for Eleanor Roosevelt that terrible winter must have had its rewards—the satisfaction of seeing her husband making his way toward partial recovery, the knowledge that he was able to keep in touch with the world outside, and sometimes, after a disagreeable session with her mother-in-law, his grateful smile. Franklin Roosevelt needed her encouragement and support that winter as he never had before and never would again, and she gave it to him in fullest measure.

15

"The Happy Warrior"

When Franklin Roosevelt returned to his New York City house on October 28, 1921, after six weeks in Presbyterian Hospital, his arms and his hands were so strong that he could grasp a leather strap suspended over his bed and turn over and move about without having to call his nurse. Also, despite Dr. Draper's gloomy prediction, life had been restored in the muscles of his back, and he could sit up. Bracing himself on his hands, he could, with some assistance, move from his bed to a wheel chair. When he said good-by to the doctors and nurses at the hospital, he assured them cheerfully: "By next spring, I'll be walking again —and without limping. Just you wait and see!"

Ahead of him, however, lay another painful ordeal. Early in January, the muscles in back of his knees began to shrink, pulling his legs up under him. Dr. Draper put his legs in plaster casts, and for two weeks he had to endure mortal agony as the doctor drove wedges in, a little deeper every day, until the muscles were stretched back. Yet in February, less than a month later, he was standing up on crutches, his legs held rigid in steel braces weighing fourteen pounds and extending from his hips down and under his feet. He was on his feet again, but he had little sense of balance and he still had to learn the difficult art of walking with braces and crutches, inching himself forward by using the muscles in his hips and back. It was a dangerous undertaking, and it required many months of patient, agonizing effort.

In April he went to Boston to be fitted with a new set of braces, and he spent the summer at Hyde Park, learning to walk. His doctors told him to get plenty of rest and to take mild, gentle exercise, but he was too impatient for that. The house at Hyde Park is set three-quarters of a mile back from the Albany Post Road, and almost every day he would try to walk from his house down to the gate. He seldom made it. Always someone would walk with him, and a servant or one of the children would follow with a wheel chair. He would laugh and talk as though it were just a stunt he was doing for pleasure, but the back of his shirt would be soaked with perspiration. His doctors said later that the effort probably did him more harm than good.

He still had his job with the Fidelity and Deposit Company of Maryland. During the winter he had conducted his business from his home, but that fall he began going to his office one, two, finally four days a week. Dr. Draper told him he had better have a wheel chair and ride from the entrance to the elevator and up to his office. But he was determined to walk, until one day one of his crutches slipped on the polished marble floor, and he went crashing down. Those who rushed forward to help him said he managed to laugh a little as with their aid he struggled back to his feet. After that he had a wheel chair meet him at the entrance. He would lunch at his desk, frequently with one of his law partners, and remain in his office until late afternoon.

Meanwhile his interest and activity in politics and civic

affairs continued to grow. During his campaign for the Vice-Presidency, he had met hundreds of state, county and city Democratic politicians, and Louis Howe had kept a list of all of them with their addresses. From time to time they would get personal, chatty letters over Roosevelt's signature, so cleverly composed by Louis Howe that they sounded as though Roosevelt had written them himself. The mailing list grew until it ran into thousands. Louis never threw away a name and address. For more than ten years, he kept those letters pouring out of New York, all over the country!

Louis was not satisfied with his own efforts. Someone close to Franklin Roosevelt would have to go out to represent him before the public. For this job, Louis selected Eleanor Roosevelt. "You'll have to get active in politics," he told her. "Since Franklin can't get around easily yet, you'll have to do it for him." Eleanor Roosevelt, who had never made a speech in her life, was appalled at the idea. To all her arguments, Louis had one question, "Do you want him to lose touch with politics, get discouraged and become an invalid?" There was only one answer. So she started going out to speak before groups of Democratic women in New York State. She was so nervous that the palms of her hands would be clammy with perspiration, her voice would become shrill and she would try to hide her embarrassment behind an odd, jerky little laugh. Louis would go along, sit in the back row and on the way home he would criticize her effort. "And for God's sake," he would say, "stop that silly giggling!" He was a hard taskmaster, but a good teacher, and eventually she became very much interested in her travels about the state. Wherever she went she would meet local politicians and invite them to New York or to Hyde Park to talk with her husband—to Mamá's obvious distaste.

Not all the work was done, however, by Mrs. Roosevelt

and Louis Howe. Even before he left Campobello, Franklin Roosevelt was dictating some letters to Missy, and the volume of his personal correspondence and the variety of his interests expanded as he grew stronger. He started a drive to offer some form of tribute to Woodrow Wilson, who at his home in Washington was slowly, but steadily losing ground in his own fight to regain his health. To one of Roosevelt's cheerful, confident letters, Wilson replied in April, 1922, "I am indeed delighted to hear that you are getting well so fast and so confidently, and I shall try to be generous enough not to envy you."

As he grew stronger and gained more confidence in his braces and crutches, Franklin Roosevelt began to appear now and then in public. He had some humiliating experiences. Once someone wrote him severely criticizing him for not rising to his feet at a meeting where a tribute was paid to the President of the United States. He replied:

"As I wear steel braces on both legs and use crutches, it is impossible for me to rise or sit down without the help of two people. . . . It is of course not exactly pleasant for me to have to remain seated during the playing of the National Anthem and on other occasions when the audiences rise, but I am presented with the alternative of doing that or of not taking part in any community enterprises whatsoever."

The Woodrow Wilson Foundation, the Walter Hines Page Memorial at Johns Hopkins University, supporting a graduate school of international relations, the drive to raise the money to build the Cathedral of St. John the Divine in New York City, the annual fund drive for the Boy Scouts of America—these were only a few of the civic enterprises in which Franklin Roosevelt played a leading part, as he slowly and painfully fought the battle to regain the use of his legs. In 1923 he drafted a plan to preserve world peace, in which he tried to remedy the defects already apparent in the League of Nations. In it he proposed an international conference to establish a new permanent organization. In other words, to kill the League of Nations and start all over again. Even then he was groping for an idea that eventually would grow into the United Nations.

He was winning his fight to lead an active, interesting life. He was becoming a man to be reckoned with in Democratic politics. Every time there was an election in his home state some newspaper or some group would propose him as the best candidate for Governor or United States Senator. His fight to walk again went more slowly, and it was costly. For three winters he spent several weeks cruising on a houseboat off the coast of Florida. He finally gave it up because he wasn't getting enough out of it to justify the expense. Despite his mother's generosity, Franklin Roosevelt was frequently very hard up during that period. More than once his wife had to wire him frantically for money to pay the servants, and several times he was obliged to sell some of his prized naval prints. Both Jimmy and Elliott were at Groton. Jimmy would soon be ready for Harvard.

Roosevelt was willing to try anything that would help strengthen the muscles of his paralyzed legs. He simply would not give up. Not until 1923 did he write the Dutchess Golf and Country Club to transfer him from active to non-resident membership. "I am still on crutches," he explained, "and cannot possibly play golf for a year or two." One thing he did learn—to move about a room alone, without his braces or crutches. He would lower himself to the floor, raise himself a little on his strong hands and arms and slide backward, dragging his useless legs. Being helpless, he had a great dread of fire. This would give him a chance to escape, he thought, if he were alone.

As the years advanced toward the middle twenties,

107

Franklin and Eleanor Roosevelt became more and more interested in the progressive Democratic Governor of New York, Alfred E. Smith. In 1922 Roosevelt persuaded Smith to run, thereby preventing the publisher, William Randolph Hearst, from getting the nomination. Roosevelt and Smith had known each other since the days when they were both in the State Legislature, and gradually had become friends. Roosevelt was unable physically to take a very active part in Smith's campaign that year, but Mrs. Roosevelt worked hard for him.

In 1924 there was a Presidential campaign, and things looked good for the Democrats, for, following President Harding's death in 1923, the Teapot Dome scandal had broken, as a result of which Harding's administration was discredited, and his Secretary of the Interior, Albert Fall, eventually went to jail, involved in dishonest dealings with some millionaire oil promoters. Harding had been succeeded by Vice-President Calvin Coolidge, who had an untainted record. Nevertheless it was doubted whether even Coolidge could pull the Republicans through if the Democrats came up with a strong candidate. It looked like a Democratic year.

The two leading candidates for the nomination for President at the Democratic National convention held in New York in July were Governor Smith and William Gibbs McAdoo, who had married Woodrow Wilson's daughter and had been his Secretary of the Treasury. Governor Smith had two strikes against him. He was a Roman Catholic, which would make him unpopular in the overwhelmingly Protestant South, where the Ku Klux Klan was running strong, and he was for repeal of the Prohibition amendment, which had been adopted right after World War I. He was also indifferent to the plight of the Middle Western farmers. The "farm problem," starting with overproduction of wheat after World War I, was to plague the nation for many, many years. Smith didn't know any farmers; he was a big city man. Roosevelt also believed that Smith was not internationally minded enough. So far as Smith was concerned, the League of Nations was a dead issue. He knew little about international politics and cared less. Nevertheless he had made a fine record as a progressive Governor of New York. Franklin Roosevelt agreed to become Smith's convention campaign manager. McAdoo, much better known throughout the country than Smith, would have a greater appeal to the anti-Catholic, "dry" voters, but his candidacy would be questioned because he had been attorney for one of the millionaires mixed up in the Teapot Dome scandal.

Old Madison Square Garden, down near Union Square in New York City, was packed to the rafters on a stifling July day, when Franklin D. Roosevelt, on crutches, his legs encased in steel braces, walked slowly and carefully to the front of the platform, handed his crutches to Jimmy, took a firm grip on the speakers' stand and gazed, smiling, out over the mass of perspiring delegates in the steaming, smoky auditorium. This was his first appearance before a large audience since he had become paralyzed.

What the audience saw was not the slender, handsome young Roosevelt it had known before. Here was a man—a big, broad-shouldered, powerful man in his very early forties. His withered legs of course were hidden behind the speakers' stand. He was still handsome, his smile warm and winning, but on his face were etched traces of the suffering he had endured, and his beautiful voice, when he started to speak, was not the voice of a young man. It had in it the resonance that only maturity can bring. The audience stared at him in silence for a split second, then broke into wild applause and cheers.

The speech Franklin Roosevelt made that day is still

regarded as one of the finest speeches ever made at a political convention. It was not filled with the flowery platitudes that make most nominating speeches tiresome. It was simple, straightforward, direct, and he had acquired a skill for which he would always be remembered by anyone who ever heard him speak. He made each person in that vast audience feel he was talking directly to him or her. Near the end he used one expression that would never be forgotten. After describing Smith's record as Governor of New York and paying tribute to his honesty and to his courage, he called him " 'The Happy Warrior' of the political battlefield."

That phrase, "The Happy Warrior," borrowed from a poem by William Wordsworth, clung to Al Smith for the rest of his life.

But the real happy warrior that day was Franklin D. Roosevelt himself. On crutches, wearing fourteen pounds of steel on his legs, he had managed to take a long, long step forward toward becoming one of this country's greatest statesmen.

16

"Dr." Roosevelt

Despite Franklin Roosevelt's valiant effort, Alfred E. Smith did not win the Democratic nomination for President in 1924. Neither did William Gibbs McAdoo. For fourteen sweltering days the convention in the old Madison Square Garden dragged on with Smith and McAdoo in a deadlock, the ballots seesawing back and forth, with Smith sometimes in the lead, sometimes McAdoo. Neither of them could muster the two-thirds majority necessary at that time for nomination. Finally on the one hundred and third ballot the weary delegates chose a compromise candidate, John W. Davis, a wealthy, conservative lawyer. He never had a chance and was easily defeated by Coolidge in the fall election.

Although his candidate did not get the nomination Franklin Roosevelt could have had practically anything he wanted from that convention. Several of the important political writers picked him as the candidate most likely to win the election if nominated, in spite of—or perhaps partly because of—his physical handicap. His gallantry, plus the fact that he was not seeking anything for himself, made him an appealing figure to the delegates, many of whom, it was said, cast longing eyes in his direction.

But Franklin Roosevelt would not have accepted the nomination. He had firmly made up his mind not to run for public office again until he had regained the use of his legs. He invited Davis and Smith to Hyde Park, persuaded Al to run for re-election as Governor of New York and went back to his search for a cure for his paralysis. He did practically nothing in the gubernatorial campaign, although his wife threw all her boundless energy into the effort to re-elect Smith, who was running against her Republican cousin, Theodore Roosevelt, Jr.

In his eagerness to get rid of his braces and crutches, Franklin Roosevelt was willing to try anything. Years later Eleanor Roosevelt said that one thing infantile paralysis taught her husband was patience. As each new type of treatment was proposed, he would give it a painstaking, thorough workout. He did not jump from one doctor to another, as some patients would. For instance, he spent many months in 1925 and 1926 working with Dr. William McDonald, a neurologist, at Marion, Massachusetts. Dr. McDonald did not believe in braces, and he undertook to strengthen the muscles in his patient's legs so he could get along without them. One phase of the treatment consisted in having Roosevelt spend two or three hours a day, dragging himself, hand-over-hand, along a railing, without his braces, trailing his shrunken legs behind him. At one point, he was able to take a few steps wearing one brace, but there the improvement stopped.

Both Dr. McDonald and Dr. Lovett in Boston had observed that swimming seemed to be of some help to polio paralytics. The difficulty was in getting water of the right temperature. In an outdoor pool, lake, or the ocean the water was too cold for the patient to stay in long enough, and the water in a heated pool was too enervating.

During the summer of 1924 Roosevelt's friend, George Foster Peabody, a banker-philanthropist, wrote him about

112

an old summer resort at Warm Springs, Georgia, in which he owned a half interest. In the meantime Roosevelt had tried out a tricycle his mother bought him and put it aside. He had also tried horseback riding, but had to give it up. Only his sense of balance kept him on the horse, which someone had to lead, at a walk. To his mother and his wife, who remembered him as a graceful, confident horseman, the sight was heartbreaking. At Warm Springs, Peabody told him, there was a pool formed by water that came gushing out of a mountain at a temperature of 88 degrees Fahrenheit. And it apparently contained some minerals that gave it buoyancy and made it less tiring than ordinary water of that temperature would be. Peabody told him about a polio patient named Louis Joseph who, after three years of swimming in that pool, was able to walk about with a cane, although he had been completely paralyzed except for his hands and arms when he arrived. There was a legend, too, that long before the white people arrived, Indians used to take their wounded braves there to recover.

Franklin Roosevelt decided to go down and have a look at the place. He left Hyde Park early in October, and his wife interrupted her work in the campaign to accompany him. What they found was an old hotel that had been a fashionable resort for wealthy Southerners before the Civil War. It had been empty for years and was falling apart. The area around the hotel and the pool was overgrown with weeds and underbrush, and the hotel was so dilapidated that it was impossible for the Roosevelts to stay there. Some friendly residents of the town turned their house over to them, along with a couple of servants. The appearance of the place was so depressing that Roosevelt must have felt like turning around and going home—until he tried the pool. Then he discovered to his amazement that he could stay in the water, exercising, for two hours without feeling tired. He began to improve at once. For the first time in three years he was able to feel some life in his toes. By the end of October he was able to walk about in water four feet deep without crutches or braces.

He tried Dr. McDonald's treatment for a couple of years and finally returned to Warm Springs. From that time on Warm Springs was Franklin Roosevelt's second home until he died there in 1945.

During one of his early visits a reporter for an Atlanta newspaper spent five days with him swimming in the pool. The reporter's article, under the heading "Franklin Roosevelt Will Swim Back to Health," was widely circulated, and before long other polio sufferers found their way to Warm Springs. At first they arrived one or two at a time, but presently they began coming in droves. They usually had no money. They had just managed to get there and that was all. Furthermore there were no places for them to stay and no doctors to examine them and decide whether they should swim or not. Many of them did not know how to swim.

Their plight was so hopeless that Tom Loyless, who had leased the property from Peabody, could see nothing to do with them except to send them home, but Roosevelt would not hear of it. He knew how desperately they needed help, and he was determined that they should have it. He persuaded a doctor from a nearby town to come over and check their hearts, make sure that they had no infectious diseases and decide whether or not it would be safe for them to swim. Makeshift housing was provided for them, and somehow they were fed, the money coming out of Roosevelt's pocket.

There was no polio specialist within many miles of Warm Springs, and those who knew about it were so skeptical that at first they refused even to visit the place. Franklin Roosevelt knew all about the exercises, for he was doing them himself every day, so he taught them to the new "patients."

114

Some of them he had to teach to swim. Before long he became known around the place as "Dr." Roosevelt, a title he may have valued more highly than any other he would ever hold.

It was inevitable of course that he should want to fix the place up, and he began pouring his own money into it. Early in 1926 he bought the place and proceeded to invest in it around two hundred thousand dollars, more than two-thirds of his personal capital. Eventually the Georgia Warm Springs Foundation was formed. It took on Roosevelt's investment as a loan. Doctors also became interested and a medical staff was set up. By 1928 Warm Springs was the most famous place in the world for the treatment of polio. And by 1928 Franklin Roosevelt was no longer on two crutches. Wearing his leg braces, he was able to walk, bending forward, with one crutch and a cane. After a time he discarded the crutch and from then on, for the rest of his life, he walked erect with one cane and the support of a strong arm. Frequently this was the arm of one of his stalwart sons. In 1928, however, he still hoped to get rid of his braces, and some of the doctors thought that, if he spent most of his time at Warm Springs for two or three more years, he might do so.

The defeat of Davis in 1924, had left the Democratic party badly shattered. The split between the conservative, "dry," anti-Catholic South and the liberal Democrats in the Northern industrial areas, who were for repeal of the Prohibition amendment and had nothing against the Catholics since, indeed, many of their leaders were Irish, had deepened and widened. The party was several hundred thousand dollars in debt with no prospect of paying it off except by obtaining big donations from wealthy businessmen, which involved an unspoken, but real, promise to "take care of them," should the Democrats win the next presidential election. Patiently, stubbornly, Roosevelt and Louis Howe went about the task of trying to bring order out of the shambles, to pull the antagonistic forces together as much as possible and to build a Democratic party which, as Roosevelt put it, "stood for something." He hated religious bigotry, but the wet-dry issue meant less to him. He wanted it to be a progressive party as opposed to Republican conservatism, and he wanted it to be an internationally-minded party. He was deeply concerned with the hope of somehow getting the nations together in an organization to prevent future wars.

Louis kept his friendly, chatty form letters flowing out to city and county leaders and plain, ordinary Democrats all over the country. Franklin Roosevelt himself took on the party's top leaders. He wrote them, met with them, pleaded and cajoled, but neither he nor Louis made much progress. In discussing possible candidates for President in 1928, many of them suggested that Roosevelt try for it, to which he firmly answered no. Alfred E. Smith was still his man. And aside from Roosevelt himself, Smith was the only man of sufficient stature to be seriously considered. It didn't look like a good Democratic year anyway. The whole country was joyously riding the Coolidge prosperity boom.

Possibly that had something to do with the fact that, after another eloquent speech by Roosevelt, Alfred E. Smith won the nomination for President on the first ballot at Houston, Texas, in June 1928.

Roosevelt was not particularly active in the presidential campaign that year. Smith obviously preferred to listen to other advisers. Mrs. Roosevelt, however, was in charge of the women's organization, working with Mrs. Belle Moskowitz, who was to Smith what Louis Howe was to Roosevelt. Smith was not an easy candidate to handle. One of his troubles was his provincialism—he seemed not to know that anything existed west of Buffalo! People in big Eastern cities, such as New York and Boston, were used to his brown derbies and his fancy shirts, his husky voice and his use of the word "raddio," for radio. They loved him, but to people in the Middle West and Far West, he looked and behaved like a vaudeville comedian, and to Southerners he was almost universally unacceptable because of his religion and his stand on prohibition.

Toward the end of the campaign the leaders became very much worried. Smith was running against Herbert Hoover, one of the most popular and respected men in the country, and he was also running against Republican prosperity. The leaders doubted that he could even carry New York State, which he would just about have to carry, with its big block of 45 electoral votes, if he were to win. He would need a strong candidate for Governor to run with him. Smith and the other leaders decided it would have to be Franklin D. Roosevelt.

Roosevelt, at Warm Springs, hopefully working with his legs, told them repeatedly that he would not do it. But they kept after him, until he finally refused to answer the telephone. When the state convention met in Rochester in September, they went to work on Mrs. Roosevelt, who had gone up to help with the women. Mrs. Roosevelt had never tried to influence her husband in making his political decisions; she refused to do so now. Finally, however, she reluctantly agreed to get her husband to the telephone so that Smith could talk to him. The call came through late, and she had to hurry to catch a midnight train back to New York, where she was teaching in a girls' private school. When her husband answered, she greeted him briefly, then silently handed the phone to Smith. As she left the room, she heard Al's husky voice saying, "Hello, Frank."

Eleanor Roosevelt read in the papers in New York the following morning that her husband was going to run for Governor of New York.

17 | Governor Roosevelt

As a campaigner, Franklin D. Roosevelt, running for Governor of New York, exceeded the expectations of Al Smith and the other party leaders. Since he had been reluctant to accept the nomination because he wanted to continue his treatment at Warm Springs, they assumed he would not be able to do much traveling. They told him he would have to make only three or four speeches. His name on the ticket would give Al all the help he needed.

Having accepted the nomination, however, Franklin Roosevelt proceeded to put on a campaign the like of which the state had not seen before. He traveled most of the time by automobile, in an open touring car with the top down. Arriving in a town—and he visited some towns no other candidate for Governor had ever bothered to visit—he would have someone straighten out his legs and lock his braces at his knees. When he was sitting down, with his knees bent, the braces had to be unlocked. His legs rigid in the braces, he would, with some assistance, get to his feet and stand erect in the rear of the car, holding onto the back of the front seat for support. He would laugh and joke as he went through this strenuous and humiliating routine, and, once he started speaking, people would forget that he was crippled. From October 17 to the end of the campaign he traveled 1,300 miles and made fifty speeches. In one day he traveled 190 miles and made seven speeches. No assignment was too tough for him. To get to the platform in one auditorium, he had to be carried, wearing his heavy steel braces, up a narrow fire escape and pulled and shoved through a window, in full view of the audience. Smiling, he straightened his tie, ran his hands over his hair and made his speech without referring to the ordeal. An admiring audience went wild in its applause.

From time to time he would refer humorously to his physical handicap. He did not like to do it, but there had been a good deal of conjecture about his health. After his first appearance at his campaign headquarters at the Biltmore Hotel in New York, one newspaper writer described him as supporting himself on the left side with a crutch and on the right side with a cane, "leaning forward on these supports so that he could draw his feet after him in a sliding gait." People wondered if a man in that condition could serve as Governor of New York.

But when Franklin Roosevelt, standing erect in the back of a car, would toss his head, grin, and ask the audience how he was doing "for a sick old man," people would roar with laughter and push forward to shake his hand. He had, they found, a warm, powerful handshake. Actually his physical handicap was more of a help than a hindrance. Human beings are quick to respond to the kind of gallantry he was showing.

On election night he went with his family to his headquarters at the Biltmore, to hear the returns. Al Smith was at the national headquarters in the General Motors building. Before 10 o'clock it had become apparent that Smith was losing. He was failing to carry New York State, and

119

some of the Southern states that had never gone Republican before had gone over to Hoover. Returns on the race for Governor came in more slowly. In those days they did not have the big computing machines used in recent elections, nor did they depend so much on radio as they would later. The returns came in over telegraph wires to the newspapers and political headquarters, where they were posted on big boards for the crowds to see.

As he sat in his headquarters at the Biltmore, mourning the defeat of Smith, it did not occur to Roosevelt that he himself might win. Louis Howe, who had not wanted him to run, fearing that, if he lost the state with Smith, it might end his political career, was heartbroken. Presently, however, returns from small towns upstate showed Roosevelt gaining a few votes here and there. But when he went home to bed at 1 A.M., Franklin Roosevelt still thought he had lost. He did not know until the next day that he had carried the state, by a slim margin of 25,000 votes. Smith had lost his own state by more than 100,000 votes. Albert Ottinger, Roosevelt's Republican opponent, demanded a re-count and waited a week before conceding defeat. During that week Roosevelt jokingly referred to himself as the "late" Governor.

When the Roosevelts moved into the big old Victorian Executive Mansion in Albany on January 1, 1929, Al Smith settled himself in a suite in an Albany hotel and waited for the new Governor to send for him. But Franklin Roosevelt, having been elected Governor, was not going to be a stooge for anyone, not even for Al Smith whom he had tried to help win the presidency. While Al waited, growing more impatient and grouchy each day, his successor went about selecting his own staff, making his own plans. Al wanted Roosevelt to retain some of his appointees. He wanted him to make Mrs. Moskowitz his secretary. Roosevelt courteously, but firmly, declined to do so. He kept only one of Smith's top officials, Miss Frances Perkins, who had a brilliant record as Chairman of the State Industrial Board, the first woman ever to hold a high appointive job in New York. Roosevelt not only kept her, he promoted her. He made her State Industrial Commissioner, in effect, Secretary of Labor for the state.

Al Smith finally gave up and returned to New York City, a morose, embittered "elder statesman." Some of his friends found a job for him, as president of the company that built, owned, and operated the new Empire State Building. He had a handsome suite of offices and a salary that must have been several times larger than any he had ever received as a public official, but he was not a happy man.

During his first two-year term as Governor, Roosevelt carried on with Smith's progressive program. As Smith had done, he fought the big electric companies that were trying to get control of the power to be developed by the proposed St. Lawrence River project. The case finally went into the courts, Roosevelt won, and the power companies gave up. There was much in Smith's program that the new Governor strongly approved. Laws protecting the rights and safety of women workers, laws against child labor, for instance, for which Miss Perkins and Mrs. Moskowitz had worked long and hard. But as he carried on with the Smith program, trying to strengthen it where he could, he began bringing out some ideas of his own. Franklin Roosevelt, who had grown up in the Hudson River valley was more interested in rural life than Smith had been. For instance, Roosevelt had learned to love trees as a child, and now he had a chance to work effectively for conservation and reforestation throughout the state.

He was interested in the problems of farmers, an interest he shared with young Henry Morgenthau, Jr., one of his

Dutchess County neighbors. Morgenthau was a farmer too. Neither he nor the Governor had ever handled a plow, milked cows, or done any of the other heavy work around a farm, but they knew about agriculture and understood the problems farmers faced. The most important farm products in New York State were milk, butter, and cheese, and the dairy farmers were in financial trouble, as were so many others all over the country. Roosevelt strongly believed that a farmer should be able to earn as good a living as anyone else. He felt that the spread between what the farmer got for his milk and what the consumer in the big cities paid for it was too great, and that something should be done about it. Morgenthau had gone to Cornell, and Governor Roosevelt made him chairman of a commission of experts from the State College of Agriculture at Cornell, to see what could be done.

Roosevelt, who liked to see things for himself, loved to travel about the state. He usually went by automobile, instructing his chauffeur not to drive faster than forty miles an hour. Forty miles an hour was then the state speed limit, and he thought the Governor should obey the law as other citizens were expected to do. One summer he took a trip across the state on his official barge *The Inspector,* following the old Erie Canal. At almost every landing his car would be waiting to take him to look over some state hospital, prison, or other institution.

Mrs. Roosevelt accompanied him on those trips and, since he could not move about easily, he would send her inside to look the place over and would invite the superintendent into his car for a drive around the grounds. He wanted to know everything! One day he asked his wife what the inmates in an institution they had just visited were getting to eat. She had copied the menus and handed them to him. "But didn't you look into the pots on the stove?" he demanded. Under his searching questions Mrs. Roosevelt

122

learned to be a thorough and accurate reporter. In addition to looking into the pots, she would open closet doors, peek into corners, pull back the covers on beds, and examine the mattresses. When it was possible, she would question the inmates, carefully watching the expressions on their faces as they talked. The result was that some state institutions which had been neglected for years got a thorough overhauling, cleaning and, where they were overcrowded, some new buildings.

Franklin Roosevelt had been Governor of New York less than a year when the "Black Friday" crash in the stock market, in October, 1929, set off the Great Depression. During the Coolidge boom, the American people, with money to spare, had started "playing the stock market," as they say in Wall Street. A buyer would purchase stocks "on margin," paying down a few dollars and owing the rest. As prices of stocks skyrocketed, he would become rich in a few days—on paper. Those who were wise sold the stocks when the price went up, paid off the balance they owed and took out their money, but most of them went right on buying more stocks on margin. By the summer of 1929 everybody was buying stocks on margin and getting rich, so they thought—cab drivers, telephone operators, housewives, doctors, who knew about medicines but not about stocks. Many of the investors had incomes so small that they could not afford to lose money on stocks or anything else. When the crash came and the bottom fell out of the market, they all lost. Even those who had enough money to pay what they owed and hold onto their stocks were ruined eventually as the prices went down and down. Some wealthy men, who should have known better, had also been playing the market, and they, too, were wiped out. Almost every day the newspapers published stories about men jumping out of office windows in the Wall Street area.

The impact at first was felt only by those who had been

playing the market and lost. The full effect would not begin to be realized for a few months, but from the first, Governor Roosevelt was worried. While President Hoover in Washington was issuing optimistic statements, and the Rockefellers were pouring money into the market to bring prices up, Roosevelt was asking himself: "Why did it happen? What can be done to prevent such a thing happening again?"

18

"People Aren't Cattle"

From the time he was elected Governor of New York in 1928, Franklin D. Roosevelt was the nation's leading potential candidate for the Democratic nomination for President of the United States. As the most important winner in an election in which his party had suffered an overwhelming and humiliating defeat, he stood head and shoulders above the other leaders.

He acted as a politician invariably acts in such a situation. He said over and over again that he was *not* a candidate for President, insisted that he was interested only in being a good Governor of New York. But he could not have failed to realize that the nomination was within his grasp. He must also have become aware that his physical handicap would not disqualify him. When he accepted the nomination for Governor, he abandoned all hope of ever again being able to walk without his leg braces. He would visit Warm Springs as often as he could for the rest of his life, but he went there for relaxation, rest, and to gain spiritual strength. From 1928 to 1932 his chief preoccupation, outside his duties as Governor, was with becoming President. To achieve this it was necessary, he knew, to do an outstanding job as Governor, he would have to be re-elected to that office in 1930 and he would have to build up a following among Democrats all around the country.

Just when he began to think of himself as a future President is a matter for conjecture. It might have been away back at Harvard as he watched the progress of his Cousin Ted's political career. He may have been serious when he made the prediction, apparently in jest, to some of his fellow law clerks as a bored young attorney in New York. Louis Howe made the prediction while Roosevelt was a fledgling State Senator in Albany, but there is no indication that Roosevelt took Louis seriously at that time. He was ambitious all right from the day he decided to run for the State Senate, and when he became Assistant Secretary of the Navy he was, of course, aware that Cousin Ted had held that job before becoming Governor of New York, Vice-President, and President. He himself at that time was ambitious to become Governor or United States Senator. As to where he hoped to go from there he told no one. Louis, of course, had an objective, but how seriously Roosevelt took Louis' plans no one knows.

If by the time he became paralyzed he had hope of some day being elected President, in spite of his defeat as candidate for Vice-President in 1920, he must have lost it temporarily in the early months of his illness. His objective then was to regain the use of his legs and to lead as active and normal a life as possible. An active and normal life for Franklin Roosevelt meant politics. Even after his glorious comeback with the "Happy Warrior" speech, he apparently thought of himself as running for office again only after he could stand and walk without braces. He had been trying for seven years to achieve that goal, with only slight success, when he first ran for Governor.

One of the first things he did after becoming Governor

in 1929 was to send a letter to all the country's prominent Democrats—former candidates, members of Congress, all delegates to the 1928 national convention, the "elder statesmen" and substantial contributors—asking them what they thought should be done to rebuild the Democratic party. The first draft of the letter was undoubtedly prepared by Louis Howe; possibly he worked with two new political advisers Roosevelt had acquired, James A. Farley, chairman of the State Boxing Commission, and a bright young lawyer named Samuel I. Rosenman, who had helped prepare some speeches during the campaign. But Roosevelt himself went over the final draft and made it his own. It was actually a form letter, so skillfully concocted that it was not tossed into the wastebasket as form letters usually are. Most of the recipients answered it, taking it very seriously indeed, giving further evidence of Roosevelt's position in the party.

While F.D.R. was Governor, Louis Howe and Jim Farley worked out of New York City, Farley acting as Roosevelt's pre-convention campaign manager, Louis continuing to send out his stream of friendly, chatty letters over Roosevelt's signature to the thousands of small fry in the Democratic party.

During his four years as Governor of New York—he was re-elected in 1930 by 800,000 votes, the largest majority that had ever been given a candidate for the job—Franklin Roosevelt was plagued by two problems. One was the Great Depression, which threw millions of New Yorkers out of work. That problem he met with courage and imagination, setting a record far above that of any other governor or the Hoover administration in Washington. The other problem was purely political, involving the careless administration of New York City's attractive and popular playboy mayor, Jimmy Walker. It stayed with him until the middle of the presidential campaign in 1932. He won out in the end, but partly by luck.

He began giving serious thought to what had caused the stock market crash right after it happened, in 1929, and how it could have been prevented. He watched carefully as the depression began spreading out over the state, and more and more heads of families began losing their jobs. His first instinct was to find means of stabilizing the situation. Several things could be done. Hours for working women could be shortened, child-labor legislation could be strictly enforced, older workers retired, and some kind of insurance or compensation, he believed, should be provided for men who lost their jobs. But at that time the cost of such a program, to be undertaken by a single state, looked prohibitive. He formed a Commission on Stabilization of Employment, made Miss Perkins chairman and asked her to keep him informed. As the number of the unemployed kept growing, he asked her for statistics, so many statistics that she could hardly keep up with him.

As wage earner after wage earner lost his job, used up his savings, let his life insurance lapse, sold his car, if he had one, for whatever he could get for it, lost his mortgaged home and finally found himself selling apples on street corners, employers and employees alike began appealing to the Governor for help. The jobless and the men who had to let them go because they could not pay them wanted action not theories. There were citizens, not so closely involved, who theorized. One theory was that booms and depressions were a natural feature of our economy, that nothing could be done about them and that the best thing to do was to let the depression hit bottom and then the economy would automatically right itself—no matter how many people had to go hungry in the meantime. Miss

Perkins was present one day when a man advocated that policy to Governor Roosevelt. In her book, *The Roosevelt I Knew,* Miss Perkins said she could never forget "the gray look of horror" on Franklin Roosevelt's face, as he said to the man: "People aren't cattle, you know."

By 1931 the unemployment situation had become so bad that Governor Roosevelt knew the state would have to act. Local communities, including the large cities, had run out of funds and were no longer able to feed the hungry. Private organizations, like the Salvation Army, could not find enough money to feed those who stood in line for hours waiting for a cup of coffee, a cup of soup, a slice of bread. So the Governor went before the Legislature and asked for $20,000,000, got it and set up the Temporary Emergency Relief Administration, which the newspapers called TERA. It was not a dole. The families on relief did not want charity, they wanted jobs. Therefore jobs of a sort were provided, mostly leaf-raking, but a man could at least keep his self-respect. At the head of TERA Roosevelt placed an imaginative, highly respected young social worker, named Harry L. Hopkins. Except for a handshake during Roosevelt's 1928 campaign, the two men had never met before. TERA was the first relief program of its kind set up in any state. It was not adequate, the Governor knew that, but it was a beginning.

This and other measures he advocated, such as unemployment insurance, made Governor Roosevelt one of the most widely discussed public officials in the country, and not only among the Democrats. In 1931 and early 1932, he was making speeches outside the state and he began to develop the technique of speaking over the radio, for which he would later become so famous.

On April 7, 1932, Governor Franklin D. Roosevelt made a speech over a radio network that may have been the first speech he made over a national hookup. In that speech he referred to the unemployed wage earner, the farmer who was losing his land by mortgage foreclosure, the small businessman who had failed because of the depression, as "The Forgotten Man." It was a phrase that would be remembered long after the rest of the speech was forgotten, as "The Happy Warrior" was. Roosevelt had by that time begun to get together his celebrated "Brain Trust," made up largely of college professors, who were to help him write his speeches and help formulate the policies he would advocate in those speeches.

At least once, the Brain Trust got him into trouble. For a speech he made in St. Paul, Minnesota, in the early spring of 1932, one of them gave him a speech almost word for word like one Al Smith, now also an avowed candidate, had made a few weeks earlier. While the whole country laughed, Louis Howe, who didn't care much for college professors, fumed about "the intelligentsias," deliberately adding the extra "s." After that, no matter how busy he was, Roosevelt would take the speech submitted to him, lie down on a couch, and, using the offering as basic material, dictate his own speech to Missy LeHand.

When the Democratic national convention met in Chicago on June 27, 1932, Roosevelt was well ahead of Al Smith in the number of votes pledged to him, but he did not yet have the two-thirds majority necessary to win the nomination. Bitter toward Roosevelt, Al, in the last few months, with his millionaire friend, the National chairman, John J. Raskob of General Motors at his elbow, had drawn closer and closer to Big Business, including the banking House of Morgan.

He and Roosevelt were the leading candidates. Off at one side, ready to become the "compromise candidate," should there be a deadlock, were: Jack Garner of Texas,

Speaker of the House of Representatives in Washington, with the 90 votes of California and Texas in his pocket; Senator J. "Ham" Lewis, the "favorite son" of Illinois, with 58 votes; Governor George White of Ohio, with his state's 52 votes. There were others, with smaller numbers of votes.

When the convention, after attending to other business, finally got around to nominating candidates for President on the evening of June 30, Governor and Mrs. Roosevelt, Mamá, John, and Elliott and two or three close friends sat by the radio in Roosevelt's study in the Executive Mansion in Albany to hear the results. In the Governor's garage telephone and telegraph wires had been strung and a radio installed for reporters for the big New York newspapers, the Associated Press, and the other wire services. They were told that the Governor was calm and cheerful, and that Mrs. Roosevelt was knitting. Anna, Jimmy, Franklin, Jr., and, of course, Louis Howe were in Chicago.

All the Roosevelts heard that night were long-winded nominating speeches and deafening demonstrations that went on and on and on. At midnight Mrs. Roosevelt served sandwiches and coffee to her family and guests and thoughtfully sent some out to the newspapermen.

It was broad daylight when the convention finally got around to taking a vote. Roosevelt led, with 666¼ ballots. He needed 770 to win. Al Smith had 201¾. Two more votes were taken that morning, with no change. Roosevelt was in the lead, but with too few votes to win. He and Smith were deadlocked. The weary delegates voted to adjourn until evening and went back to their hotels to get some sleep.

When they assembled again that evening rumors were going about that a "deal" had been made. These rumors proved to be correct. After the crowd had quieted down, William Gibbs McAdoo walked onto the platform and announced that Garner was turning his 90 votes over to Roosevelt. That started the band wagon rolling, and Governor Franklin D. Roosevelt of New York was nominated on the first ballot, the fourth of the convention. Jack Garner was then nominated for Vice-President.

The following day Governor Roosevelt did something no other candidate for President had ever done. The custom was for the candidate to be formally notified of his nomination with appropriate ceremonies two or three weeks after the convention, but Roosevelt, his wife, and his sons Elliott and John flew out to Chicago in a small bumpy plane, and that afternoon he appeared before the convention.

No one who was there that afternoon will ever forget the thunder of applause he got as he said in ringing tones: "I pledge you, I pledge myself, to a New Deal for the American people."

19

Conquering Hero

Back in Albany, acclaimed by press and public for his stirring acceptance speech, with the strains of "Happy Days Are Here Again" still ringing in his ears, Franklin Roosevelt had to face up to the second of the problems that had ridden him all through his two terms as Governor of New York.

The first one, unemployment growing out of the Great Depression, he had met with understanding and imagination far beyond that shown by any other governor or by the Hoover administration. The second one was what to do about Jimmy Walker, Mayor of New York City. It must be solved before he could start on his big campaign swing around the country.

Early in 1929, at the beginning of his first term as Governor, Louis Howe had warned Roosevelt that the Walker administration was riddled with corruption. Rumors of corruption in and around City Hall were so widespread and so persistent that most New Yorkers seemed to take them for granted. But they did not care, due to the popularity of the gay, witty, debonair Jimmy. It was the age of jazz and speak-easies, where liquor was served illegally because of the Prohibition amendment. Speak-easies flourished all around the city and nobody bothered about them. Against the drab background of the depression, Jimmy Walker, who looked and acted more like a movie star than a mayor, was at least refreshing. The great majority of the people in New York City loved him.

Even in New York City, however, there were some sober, thoughtful, and distinguished citizens who believed, as Roosevelt believed, in honest government. Their spokesman was former Judge Samuel Seabury, an anti-Tammany Democrat. And the Republicans, who didn't count in New York City, but who controlled the State Legislature, were naturally out after Jimmy Walker's scalp.

In the fall of 1929 New York City held a municipal election, with Walker running against a man who would himself become years later one of the most popular mayors New York City ever had, Fiorello La Guardia. All through the campaign La Guardia hammered away at corruption in the Walker administration, even citing names. But Jimmy Walker carried the city by 200,000 votes. La Guardia was so badly beaten that on election night he closed up his headquarters at 8 o'clock and went home.

By 1929 Franklin Roosevelt had become a shrewd, experienced politician. Any smart politician knows that to get anywhere with his program, however worthy it may be, he must first win his party's nomination and get himself elected to office. Roosevelt, with his eye on the White House, knew that he must be elected to a second term as Governor of New York. Should he fail, he was finished. If Tammany, infuriated by any action he took against Jimmy Walker, blocked his nomination at the state convention, he could not even run for re-election. He couldn't take that chance. He had too much to lose.

Meanwhile Jimmy Walker, after his thumping victory,

grew more and more careless, spending less time at City Hall, leading parades, making after-dinner speeches, going to parties. His public utterances were anything but profound, but they were always amusing. Most New Yorkers loved his elaborate wardrobe and enjoyed, vicariously, his gay, carefree life. He had expensive tastes. He owned a house in Greenwich Village, but he spent most of his time in a suite in a swank hotel at Park Avenue and 65th Street, right across the street from the Roosevelt town house. The kind of entertaining he did there certainly could not be condoned by Seabury or Roosevelt—or by Al Smith, for that matter—and Seabury and his group kept asking where he was getting the money to live that way.

It required much patience and political fortitude, but Governor Roosevelt withheld his fire until he had been nominated and re-elected—even as the reformers lambasted him and called him "wishy-washy." Once he was re-elected, Roosevelt moved. Early in 1931 he signed a bill authorizing a $500,000 legislative investigation of Jimmy and his administration. To Walker, he issued a stinging public warning:

"Our little Mayor can save much trouble in the future by getting on the job, cleaning his own house and stopping wisecracks. If he does not do all this, he can have only himself to blame if he gets into trouble."

With Judge Seabury as chief counsel, the legislative hearings in New York City dragged on for fourteen months and came up with 69,000 pages of testimony, most of it devastating to Walker. Roosevelt forwarded the evidence to him and demanded a reply. When Walker finally complied, after weeks of delay, his answers were as weak and evasive as they had been at the hearings. The Governor directed Jimmy to appear before him in person in Albany on August 11.

135

Judge Seabury presented the evidence. Roosevelt asked the questions. For three weeks the hearings went on, while Roosevelt delayed his big campaign trip. Coldly courteous, he asked Jimmy Walker one embarrassing question after another about his personal finances: How was it that a clerk in his old law office was paying the Mayor's bills out of a deposit of $961,000 in one bank? Why had a taxicab holding company given him $26,000 in bonds? How did he happen to get $246,000 in split-stock profits from a publisher without putting up a dime? Walker, fidgeting in his chair on the other side of the desk, had only one answer: He had generous friends. Was there anything wrong in that?

The newspapers, in New York and all over the country, carried columns and columns on the hearings. But the so-called "man in the street" in New York City seemed to pay little attention. The first week's hearings ended late Friday afternoon, and Jimmy, riding in the private car of one of his rich friends, took a train to New York for the week end. As he arrived in Grand Central Station, he was greeted by a little German band, playing, incongruously, "Happy Days Are Here Again," and as he walked up the long ramp into the rotunda, girls dressed in white danced ahead of him, strewing rose petals in his path. To some New Yorkers, at least, the dapper Jimmy was still a hero.

The hearings had been in progress for three weeks, and Governor Roosevelt, impatient to get on with his campaign, had started holding evening sessions, when they adjourned one Friday afternoon. It had been a bad day for Jimmy, squirming under the Governor's relentless questions. As he strode down the hill from the Capitol, he stormed to a reporter, "I always knew Frank Roosevelt was a bum lawyer, but I thought he could at least be fair." The Governor had not been unfair. Jimmy was in serious trouble, and he knew it.

That day turned out to be the last day of the hearings. The sessions were supposed to be resumed on Monday, but were postponed because of a death in the Walker family. On the evening of September 1, in his study in the Executive Mansion, Roosevelt was hotly arguing with a group of Walker supporters who wanted him to let the little Mayor off, when someone handed him a telegram. The telegram informed him that Jimmy Walker had resigned as Mayor of New York. Roosevelt was relieved of the necessity to make any decision. And whatever damage his stern questioning of Walker may have done to him among the voters in New York City, it had raised his stature all over the rest of the country. Some of the politicians called it "Roosevelt luck."

The Brain Trust had been busily engaged preparing speeches for him, but Roosevelt had to go over them and make them his own. Finally on the night of September 12 he left Albany on his long delayed big campaign swing, a trip which many of his advisers thought he should not attempt because they doubted his ability to take the physical punishment. They didn't really know their man.

He was away a little less than a month, returning to Albany on October 8. During that time he had traveled almost 9,000 miles, had made fifteen important speeches, had made countless back platform appearances on the arm of his "little boy Jimmy," as he called him, and showed no signs of fatigue whatsoever. Political experts were unanimous in predicting his election, as President Hoover, appearing weary and depressed, hopelessly tried to defend his administration.

Roosevelt made his first important speech—he may have regarded it as his most important speech—in Topeka, Kansas, on a blistering hot day. Standing on the steps of the state capitol, he faced an audience variously estimated at from 18,000 to 25,000 wheat farmers, grim-faced, deeply

137

tanned, in faded, ragged clothes. They stared intently at a tall man, with big, powerful shoulders. As usual, his legs were concealed behind the speaker's stand, on which he kept a firm grip with one hand. He was tanned too, and he frequently wiped his forehead, for perspiration trickled down from his rumpled hair. His clothes were casual, loose-fitting and somewhat wrinkled, as they always were because of his braces. He said he was a farmer, too, and he looked like a farmer, although he was not ragged, as they were.

He talked like a farmer, too, in language they understood in spite of his Harvard accent. He offered them no pedantic economic theories. His program was still in the making, and he told them he would be glad to receive their suggestions. A way must be found so that a farmer could earn as good a living as anyone else. His program, he said, should be administered, as far as possible, at the local level by the farmers themselves. It should be voluntary, with no coercion from Washington. The Hoover administration had suggested that the wheat farmers, to cut down overproduction, allow 20 per cent of their land to lie idle, without any recompense for the farmer. This Roosevelt described as "a cruel joke."

In the broiling sun, his audience listened in silence. They did not cheer; they did not applaud. They just stood and listened. Hoover had done nothing for them. Would this man help them? Could he? Nobody on the train that night could guess what those farmers were thinking. Roosevelt regarded all his farm speeches—and he made several more, in Nebraska, Iowa, and Wisconsin—as more important than any others he made. In the big farm belt, in the center of the country, the voters were traditionally Republican. Roosevelt thought he could win them, and, as it turned out, he did.

From Topeka to Denver, to Salt Lake City, to Butte,

Montana, Portland, and Seattle, San Francisco, Los Angeles, Omaha, Sioux City, Iowa, Milwaukee, Chicago, Detroit, with hundreds of brief stops in between, he traveled. Power control, the rights of labor, better working conditions, some form of unemployment insurance, relief for the unemployed—the speeches were all about matters in which the voters were deeply interested. Sometimes he attacked Hoover's policies, but mostly he talked about what he would do if he were elected.

In some of the larger cities, in Chicago, for instance, big demonstrations were put on, whipped up by the party bosses, but most of the audiences were not particularly demonstrative. They just listened. He got some of his best reactions from the crowds that gathered around the train, when he would walk out onto the rear platform and make what the newspapermen called his "little boy Jimmy" speech, laughing and joking with the people, shaking hands with as many as could reach him.

On his return from the Western trip, his advisers told him it shouldn't be necessary for him to do any more traveling, but he did make shorter trips, into the Middle West, to the South, and up into New England. On the day before the election he toured his home county, stopping at grocery stores and post offices.

"You'd think," a member of his party remarked, "that he was running for the State Senate and had to carry Dutchess County to win!"

On election night the candidate went to the Hotel Biltmore to hear the results. He did not have to wait very long. When he went to the hotel ballroom around midnight to thank his deliriously happy campaign workers, two strange men had joined his party. They were Secret Service men, assigned to guard the future President of the United States!

Index

141

LORENA A. HICKOK

Born in Wisconsin, as a reporter for over twenty years Lorena A. Hickok covered everything from politics to the Lindbergh kidnaping, from society to football. She worked for the Minneapolis *Tribune,* the old New York *Tribune,* the Milwaukee *Sentinel,* and the Associated Press, handled promotion for the 1939 New York World's Fair, and has been an executive secretary of the Women's Division, Democratic National Committee.

Ill health forced her retirement in 1945, since which time she has written six books for young people, the most recent being *The Touch of Magic,* the biography of Anne Sullivan Macy (Dodd Mead, 1961). Miss Hickok lives in the Village of Hyde Park, New York.